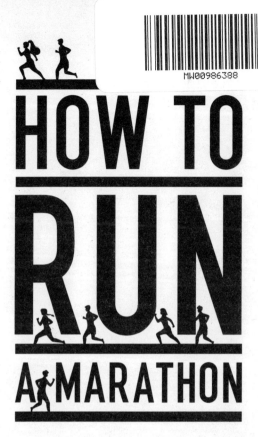

HOW TO
RUN
A MARATHON

VASSOS ALEXANDER

HOW TO RUN A MARATHON

THE GO-TO GUIDE FOR ANYONE AND EVERYONE

HarperCollins*Publishers*

While the author of this work has made every effort to ensure that the information contained in this book is as accurate and up-to-date as possible at the time of publication, medical knowledge is constantly changing and the application of it to particular circumstances depends on many factors. Therefore, it is recommended that readers always consult a qualified medical specialist for individual advice. This book should not be used as an alternative to seeking specialist medical advice, which should be sought before any action is taken. The author and publishers cannot be held responsible for any errors and omissions that may be found in the text, or any actions that may be taken by a reader as a result of any reliance on the information contained in the text which is taken entirely at the reader's own risk.

HarperCollins*Publishers*
1 London Bridge Street
London SE1 9GF

www.harpercollins.co.uk

HarperCollins*Publishers*
1st Floor, Watermarque Building, Ringsend Road
Dublin 4, Ireland

First published by HarperCollins*Publishers* 2021

10 9 8 7 6 5 4 3 2 1

A catalogue record of this book is available from the British Library

ISBN 978-0-00-837722-9

Printed and bound in Great Britain by CPI Group (UK) Ltd, Croydon

MIX
Paper from
responsible sources
FSC www.fsc.org **FSC® C007454**

This book is produced from independently certified FSC™ paper to ensure responsible forest management.

For more information visit: www.harpercollins.co.uk/green

This book is dedicated to you – and every start line you cross.
May the journey bring you joy.

CONTENTS

PROLOGUE – BARCELONA

'Our running shoes have magic in them: the power to transform
a bad day into a good day, frustration into speed, self-doubt
into confidence, chocolate cake into muscle.'
Mina Samuels, author

I suppose it's too late to back out of this, but I tell you what, I'm bloody tempted.

I'm one of 11,000 people crammed behind the start line of the 2011 Barcelona marathon and I very much expect I'm about to get found out. I've not done the proper training. I wanted to, but I've been injured. And also, let's face it, I'm not a real runner. Unlike every single person surrounding me, fit, athletic, toned, making last-second adjustments to shoelaces, shorts, expensive watches. They're obviously proper runners. Not me.

I began to feel like an imposter in the hotel breakfast room first thing. They'd opened especially early for us marathon runners ('us runners' – ha!) and while I dithered and nervously nibbled at a stale croissant, the others were all piling into the porridge, merrily munching on muesli and greedily guzzling granola. A fitter and more focused collection of people you could never hope to see milling around a breakfast buffet. They terrified me.

None of this did I convey to my cousin, also named Vassos, who was sitting opposite, beaming with excitement. He'd done all the training, and more. Also, importantly, he'd already run four marathons. He knew he had this. I watched as he wandered off languidly to toast more bread. He fitted in perfectly.

Indeed the only question in my cousin's mind that morning was what time would he run? By contrast, questions churning around in my head included:

Will I have to stop and walk? (Probably)
Will I finish? (Probably not)
How mortifying would it be not to finish? (Very)
How far until it hurts?
Will I even last a mile on my dodgy knee?
What does 'The Wall' feel like?
Do I honestly want to know?
What if I'm last?
What happens if I can't continue?
Will the people of Barcelona laugh at me?
Is there sufficient medical cover?
Why am I doing this?
And mostly, how can I possibly, **possibly** *need another poo?*

Of all the pre-race surprises assailing my thoughts and senses, by far the most shocking is how often I seem to need the loo. Surely by now there's simply nothing left? I go for a third time straight after breakfast, a fourth before leaving the hotel room. And as we emerge into milky Barcelona sunshine, I dive back into reception for 'No. 2' number five.

Almost 100 marathons and ultra-marathons later, I do still feel compelled to do multiple pre-race poos. The maranoia, on the other hand – that strange, hypochondriacal pre-race madness that affects marathon runners (and drives their friends and family potty) that's largely gone, I'm pleased to say. But in Barcelona it was all-consuming.

In fact, those questions churning around my mind on the start line are the culmination of a fortnight of fretting. For two weeks, every walking step has seemed to aggravate a different body part. I've had trouble sleeping through the aches, pains and niggles. I even ruined a family weekend in Bath, sulking because I was convinced my ankle was about to implode. All pure maranoia.

And speaking of potty, I wonder briefly if the problem in my bowels is down to something I ate last night. Cousin Vassos and I had inadvertently invented a private, marathon-eve tradition as we wandered into a city centre restaurant in search of carbs. It was the sort of place we imagined Catalan locals dined at for special occasions. That's probably exactly the vibe they were hoping tourists would feel, and it worked a treat. We were seated in the middle of a busy yet understated dining room, ordered a beer each and cheerfully asked our waiter to bring whatever food he suggested would help the two of us run a good race the following morning.

I'm not sure the waiter was well schooled in the delicate art of marathon nutrition, but he certainly knew how to lay on a proper feast. Dish after wonderful dish was laid before us, all colourful, all bursting with flavour, all dripping in oil, like nothing we'd ever eaten before. After a brief moment considering the wisdom of eating these new concoctions on the eve of a big race, we decided to simply relax and go with the flow.

Well, what a flow! Massive plates of pork, snails, onions, smoked sardines, seafood paella, even oxtail with foie gras. This was before I went plant-based, obvs. We revelled in the thrill of ignoring all the sensible advice we'd ever been given about eating a tried-and-tested, simple supper the night before a marathon. *Don't risk running with an upset stomach*, they say. We both went high-risk in Catalunya that night.

Not that we knew it at the time, but Barcelona was to be the first of many one-night European odysseys – fly somewhere on a Saturday, run a marathon the following morning, home by Sunday evening. And from Bergen to Copenhagen, Ljubljana to Prague, we searched out the most eclectic restaurant to gorge ourselves on local delicacies, the weirder the better. We knew that one day we might live to regret it, but the risk only added to the enjoyment.

No risk of any enjoyment on the Barcelona start line. Nerves are so loud they're verging on panic.

The man on the public address system starts the countdown. Oh God, now I urgently need a wee. I have a matter of seconds to consider this latest setback before the hooter sounds. The marathon is underway! Around me, everyone starts shuffling forwards towards the start line. I'm in with the group expecting to finish in around 3:30 – only because I followed my cousin in here – and in the few minutes it takes to reach the start, I make a snap decision to remove the timing chip from my shoe and discard it. If I'm going to fail here, and let's face it, I probably am, ain't nobody gonna know about it.

Whenever I've needed to pee mid-race since, I think back to those opening few yards in Barcelona. As we all started running and I was flipping the timing chip to the side of the road, my bladder felt full to bursting. By the time we'd reached the first bend in the road, it was as if I'd never needed to go at all. I'm pretty sure I didn't wet myself in the meantime. So either, I thought, this whole urge to wee was psychosomatic, or my body modified the signals it was sending to my brain because it knew bigger problems now lay ahead: 26.2 of them.

Though actually, around two-thirds of those went gloriously smoothly.

I'd been looking forward to passing the famous Camp Nou stadium, home to FC Barcelona, and was thrilled to discover the route went right around it. And five miles done already.

I was also pleased that the Sunday morning streets were relatively quiet. Loads of cheering Catalans would emerge later but they'd do so, quite rightly, in their own good time. Which meant to me that there were fewer people to witness my inevitable disgrace as I pulled out of the race.

My long runs in training had built up to 16 miles, but no further. The planned 18- and 20-mile runs in my 17-week plan were abandoned due to a dodgy ankle. It also put paid to all running for the past month.

As it turns out, 16 miles in training with a month-long taper gets you through 18 miles of a marathon in good order.

I'm resolute. I'm focused. I'm enjoying myself. I've long since stopped fretting about anything and everything, and – whisper it quietly – I almost feel like I belong here. In fact, as a Greek, I'm allowing visions of Pheidippides to fill my head.

Now in case your ancient Greek history is a little rusty, let me briefly remind you about Pheidippides. He's the heroic ancient Greek messenger whose fault all this is, basically. If it weren't for him, you definitely wouldn't be reading a book called *How to Run a Marathon*. And I'd be a lot less sweaty generally. I wonder what we'd all be doing instead.

In 490 BC, Pheidippides ran from Marathon to Athens, around 26 miles, to deliver news of a near-miraculous victory in battle against the Persians.

I'm colouring in his epic journey as I pass the 18-mile marker in Barcelona. I'm imagining the nascent Greek democracy and the state of dread and fear Pheidippides would have been running home to. He had joyful but urgent information. If the massed ranks of invading Persians had won, which by rights they ought to, then they planned to subjugate the Greeks and destroy their civilisation. In Athens, the only option would be to set fire to the city and head for the hills. Democracy as we know it would have died in its infancy.

But somehow the Greeks prevailed and our hero needed to get word home before his fellow citizens did anything rash.

Now poor old Pheidippides had been having quite a week of it. He'd already run 300 miles to Sparta and back, unsuccessfully, begging for help. And he'd doubtless fought in the bloody battle as well. So, 26-odd miles later, when he arrived back in Athens to deliver his victorious message, the poor chap collapsed and died of understandable exhaustion. But the marathon was born.

I'm hoping for an equally jubilant, but rather less fatal, conclusion to my first-ever marathon. And I've got to say, so far, so good. I've come two miles further than I've ever run in my life and I'm still feeling strong. Also – this comes as a massive surprise – I appear to be keeping pace with the runners around me. Cousin Vassos may have disappeared up the road, but the 3:30 pacer is still around here somewhere. I begin to believe that everything might actually be okay. I won't just finish, but finish well.

Then everything starts to unravel.

A man directly in front of me stops running and pulls to the side of the road, clutching his hamstring flamboyantly. It serves as a trigger. After that, most things in my body begin to hurt and my legs feel like they're running through treacle.

Beautiful monuments come and go: the magnificent Sagrada Família cathedral, a century in the making and still unfinished; the long, tree-lined promenade Las Ramblas; the Port of Barcelona, with its yachts, ferries and container ships. But I'm largely oblivious, wrapped up in my troubles. Fleeting thrill, running through the huge, ornate Arc de Triomf, then straight back to fretting about my Bambi legs.

Other runners are streaming past me now, and I seem to be running in slow motion. I'm giving it everything, but suspect I may be even going backwards. I notice the route is passing the open doorway of our hotel. I imagine myself back inside, perhaps in a bath enjoying a well-earned beer. It *would* be well earned too. After all, I've run further than ever before. Surely there'll be other opportunities to

complete a marathon. I should celebrate the 20-plus miles
I've managed, not lament the few that got away. Simply stop
running, and start running a bath …

Major realisation number one: nobody would care if I
surrendered now. Literally nobody. Not my cousin, not my
wife or young children, not any of my friends.

Major realisation number two: I'd care. Dammit. I'd care
a lot.

Conclusion: I'm finishing this. Somehow, if at all possible,
I'm finishing.

It's actually rather liberating. Take 'give up' off the menu,
and all that's left is 'carry on'.

Every footstep now feels like an event. Runners stream
past in their hundreds. But I'm locked into my determination
and refuse to be dispirited. I discover something about myself
through those painful, laboured miles. It's since become the
biggest weapon at my disposal: a simple willingness to just
keep going. Even when the finish line seems impossibly far
away, on legs that will surely implode any second … Just.
Keep. Going.

Another six miles seems inconceivable, preposterous. But
another six paces doesn't. So I break down the distance, get
to the next water station, mile marker, street corner, tree …
And go again.

Eventually it dawns on me that there's only a mile or so to
go and I allow myself to believe that I'll finish. I could crawl
home from here. I calculate that my current, glacial rate of
progress will see me come in just outside the four-hour mark.

And suddenly I'm Popeye after a can of spinach. I find a
little burst of, well, not speed exactly, but certainly increased

pace. I cross the line just as the excitable announcer tells the now-crowded start/finish area that everyone's been running for four hours exactly.

If you're being kind, my gun time is 3:59:59. I don't have a chip time because I threw away my chip in the morning panic. My stopwatch says 3:56:01.

I see my cousin waiting on the far side of the square. I try to wave but my arm refuses to move. The tiredness is exquisite. I have just completed a marathon.

Yes, it's been done before. But not by me.

And now it's your turn.

INTRODUCTION

'Doubt kills more dreams than failure ever will.'
Suzy Klassem, poet

It's become traditional to begin a running book with tales of extreme physical torment. 'Show, don't tell' is the accepted wisdom. So what you do is describe – in as much detail as you dare – your lowest ebb in a particularly arduous race. The moment you thought you couldn't go on, when you simply could not take another single step, could barely even summon the energy to breathe … And you leave it there, hanging.

And then, at the very end of the book, in the final pages of the final chapter, you return to the scene and describe how somehow, bravely, against all the odds, you found a way. You endured. Miraculously, you succeeded. You're a hero! (I may have been guilty of using this technique myself once or twice. Okay, twice.)

However, let's begin *How to Run a Marathon* with a nice sit down on your comfiest, squishiest sofa. You're probably watching the telly and eating crisps. (I was.) You may have a glass of wine or a bottle of beer in your hand. And you may even pop outside for the occasional sneaky cigarette. (I did.)

Maybe it's a springtime Sunday morning as you lounge on that tempting sofa of yours and it's the London Marathon you're watching on TV. You can't fail to be uplifted by those spectacular athletes vying for victory in the women's and men's elite and wheelchair races. And perhaps even more so by the 40,000 amateur runners who follow them onto the streets of London every year and the millions who turn out to cheer them on.

I always think if an alien were to land on our planet and wonder where to go to see the best of us, the Embankment on London Marathon Sunday morning would be just about perfect. All that fitness and determination inside the barriers. All that money being raised for good causes. All those tidal waves of goodwill washing over the runners from the throngs of spectators a dozen deep on both sides of the road. And not forgetting the brilliant volunteers who support, inspire and smile as they staff the aid stations.

But are you feeling, as I most certainly did, that running marathons is something other people do? I mean, for goodness' sake, 26.2 miles? I'd often think twice about driving that far in a car.

However I'm here to tell you that running a marathon will change your life. For the better, obviously. And I'm also here to tell you that you CAN do it.

I promise it'll be hard. It wouldn't be worthwhile if it wasn't. But I promise you won't regret it.

You know perhaps I got it wrong in my other books. The miracle is not that I managed to finish that ridiculously difficult race. The miracle is that I dared to start running in the first place. The first step is always the hardest.

During the coronavirus pandemic, when much of the world was in lockdown, millions discovered running. There were no races to train for. There was no sport on TV to inspire. Marathons were cancelled. And yet people who'd never previously considered running were lacing up trainers in their droves and using their allotted daily exercise to find out what all the fuss was about. As one UK newspaper put it at the time, perhaps the London 2012 Olympics had it wrong with the motto 'Inspire a Generation'. People don't become active when there's hour after hour of thrilling action on their tellies. Instead they sit on their backsides and watch it. 'Imprison a Generation', on the other hand, and they can't wait to start running!

And when you do start running, there's one finish line with a lure like no other: the marathon.

I'm not the fastest or most elegant runner. Far from it. My right knee collapses inwards, sending the ankle flailing out and posing a danger to passers-by. I've never run competitively nor coached anyone above school age. The closest I've come to a marathon world record is lunch with Paula Radcliffe. So in many ways I'm precisely the wrong person to be writing this book. Except that I'm not. Because when it comes to enjoying marathon running, appreciating it, being grateful for it ... I'm world class.

PART ONE

WHY EVERYONE SHOULD DO IT

MANCHESTER

Fall down seven times. Get up eight.
Japanese proverb

The morning dawns bright and beautiful. The sky has been painted by Turner, every conceivable shade of yellow. It's what Mark Twain called one of those rich, rare spring days when it is heaven to be out of doors. Which is just as well, because many thousands of us will be outside all morning. It's the day of the Manchester Marathon.

I'm fit and excited, but feeling no pressure whatsoever. I'm aiming for a good time in London later this month; this is merely a happy training run.

There's something magical crackling in the air like electricity as we walk to the start in the shadow of Old Trafford – the famous old Theatre of Dreams providing the backdrop to our own running dreams: a first marathon finish, loads of money raised for a wonderful cause, perhaps even an elusive PB.

There's the magic again as runners chat excitedly in the (relatively short) queue for the loo. And as we count down expectantly to the 9 a.m. start time, you can feel it, taste it, almost touch it.

The atmosphere as we begin running is immense. It seems everybody in the city has turned out to cheer us away – every single one of them smiling. It's infectious. 20,000 runners are grinning too as we embark on a three-mile tour of Trafford before the route takes us under the M60 and south towards Sale. They call this the 'fast, flat and friendly marathon' and they're not wrong on any count. Friendliness spills over the barriers and onto the course. It's life-affirming. My shoulder almost starts aching with all the high fives.

We continue south to Timperley, where we're welcomed by a raucous Rock Choir and locals offering bananas, jelly babies and boundless goodwill. Several families have created impromptu aid stations in front of their houses.

As we enter the tumultuous centre of Altrincham, the sheer 'fastness' of the course is reinforced. There's an incline. It's not long and it's definitely not steep, but it comes as a bit of a shock. Because in 12 miles, the closest we've come to anything resembling a hill is a little railway bridge.

In fact it's quite refreshing to be using some different muscles for a minute or so, and then, gravity being what it is, what goes up must come down. We enjoy the benefit of a gentle descent as we saunter through halfway.

I run a few miles alongside a friendly chef called Matt. We talk running times. What else? It soon becomes clear he's running easier than me. I still have my sights set on London, so as soon as it becomes an effort to keep chatting, I let him go. Checking the results later, I'm thrilled to see he's set a new

PB of 2:56. He didn't slow at all in the second half of the race, a trick I've literally never managed to pull off.

Meanwhile, I'm having a ball. I've run enough marathons by now to be able to knock off the distance relatively routinely. It only really hurts if I'm trying for a particular time. And today, the prospect of suffering never even occurs to me. Every time it starts to sting, I ease back into my comfort zone.

I start observing the other runners. At the very front of the field, everyone looks the same. They all run with the graceful elegance of children. Nice, high ankle lift and a strong, upright gait. Occasionally, you might see a nodding head like Paula Radcliffe's, but if you look beyond that, the legs and torso are perfect. Underneath that famous grimace, even Emil Zátopek looked like he ran in famously velvet shoes.

Back with me, however, there's all manner of weirdness. The Shufflers barely lift their feet. The Thumpers hit the ground really hard. I'm more of an Octopus: arms and legs all over the place. However much I like to think I'm gliding along serenely, a glance at my right leg puts me firmly in my place. The knee collapses inwards and the ankle flails. I once had my gait analysed in 3D in a lab near Oxford. They put clever sensors all over my body and set me going on the treadmill. In my mind I was running with the poise and grace of a thoroughbred racehorse; I was looking forward to much accolade and kudos. The results were gravely disappointing. It's a wonder runners like me can run 26.2 miles at all, let alone in under seven minutes-a-mile.

If we all ran 'perfectly' – think Mo Farah or Eliud Kipchoge – we'd sustain fewer injuries. There's also evidence that keeping our heads up as we run, thus fully stretching our body's fascia system, gives us free, elastic energy with every step. However, as later discussed in Stretching and Injury Prevention, it's equally fine to run however we naturally run and just make the most of that.

Then there's the marathon soundtrack. Venture deep into the field and all you'll hear is wheezing, puffing, coughing and gasping. Occasionally, a particularly heavy breather will materialise just behind you and the noises they're emanating make you concerned for their wellbeing. You want to ask if they're okay, suggest they take a break. But just a tiny bit too, you want to run faster to get away, because it is, frankly, a little disgusting.

Which brings us onto all the spitting and nose blowing. To run a big city marathon is often to run a gauntlet of bodily excretions. You never quite know when someone running next to you might need to spit and whether a globule might be heading towards your face as you run.

Or, worse, a bogey missile. We're all guilty occasionally of blowing our noses on the run. I try to make sure there's nobody around me when I do. Nobody in sight preferably, though that's obviously tricky mid-marathon. I once suffered the severe misfortune, at mile 21 of the otherwise magnificent Beachy Head Marathon, of somebody's snot landing in my open mouth. The woman in question was above me on a steep climb and forcefully blew her nose over her shoulder. Fierce wind whipped the resultant slime into my mouth. She was exceptionally apologetic. I was not especially magnanimous.

Other flying missiles to have hit me during marathons include water bottles at aid stations and old clothes being jettisoned near the start. Most runners do take care to avoid fellow competitors when they lob stuff away. You take the occasional hit and carry on.

No such troubles today in Manchester. I'm grinning broadly as I run the final mile down Talbot Road to the finish in Lancashire County Cricket Club. I'm going to finish a minute or two outside three hours and I've had a whale of a time. However, all around me are the dejected faces of runners who've given everything to break the magical three-hour barrier and have come up just short. It's a feeling I've known only too well. But this is a year or two after I finally managed to run 2:59, and today everything's gone smoothly. I've run within myself, never allowed myself to suffer, and I'm beaming. A pal watching from the roadside tells me I look like the one happy idiot in a sea of misery.

As I collect my medal, still smiling, I bump into Dani Nimmock, elite runner and head of exhibitions at London Marathon Events. She's just won the women's race and shattered her PB. Understandably elated, she asks how I got on.

'Breezed around in 3:02. Loved it. Took my foot off the gas every time it started feeling tough.'

Dani looks at me, astonished.

'Why?'

And then the penny drops.

It was the perfect day and the perfect course for a PB. The weather was fresh and still, conditions could not have been kinder. My legs were impeccable. Frankly, how often do marathons *ever* feel this easy? Suddenly I find myself wishing I'd given it the full monty and fervently wondering what might have been.

For us amateurs, marathon running is an elaborate game. It's a game we play earnestly and vigorously, but it's definitely a game. It has echoes of the games of our child-hoods, how seriously we would play them, how unpredictable they were.

Same with a marathon. You never really know how a marathon will turn out until quite near the end. Today, in Manchester, perhaps I played the wrong game. I did have fun, but spurned the chance of a PB. Then again, who knows? If I'd really gone for it, added pressure, more stress, perhaps I'd have run even slower. A few weeks later, in the hottest London Marathon ever, a PB was never on.

And so the game continues. It really is a smashing game and we're lucky to play it.

THE WOMAN WHO FINISHES LAST

'We are all runners, some just run faster than others.
I never met a fake runner.'
Bart Yasso, *Runner's World* Chief Running Officer

Lisa Jackson is ace. A veteran of over 100 marathons, she's the author of *Your Pace or Mine?*, a running book every bit as good as its title. Lisa's widely known in running circles for her floppy flamingo hat, for meeting new people and chatting during races, and for frequently finishing stone last. Like I say, she's ace. Exactly the sort of person running needs. You can now catch up with her latest exploits in her column for *Runner's World* magazine. When we met to chat about what marathon running means to her, in the beautiful courtyard cafe at the V&A museum in London, we were sitting at a table next to some noisy art students. But they went quiet as Lisa started to talk, apparently inspired to listen in…

Speed isn't the only way to measure your running success. If I had to measure my running success by speed, I'd be a total failure because

I've come last in 25 marathons. I came to the conclusion that I don't need to worry what anyone else thinks of me, I just need to be a hero in my own life.

I didn't start running until I was 30. I had two really very fit parents and I think it was a bit embarrassing when we went on holiday that they would knock out a half-marathon before breakfast and I'd still be asleep by the time they came back. Once I spent the entire Christmas on the couch eating Stilton out of a jar with a spoon, drinking port. And I just didn't like myself very much, sitting on that sofa. It didn't feel right. So I started running.

When I go to a marathon, I measure my performance by how many people I've spoken to, how many people I've helped and encouraged when they were feeling terrible. If I've managed to run in amazing scenery, that to me is an achievement as well, cause it's obviously more challenging than running on a road. If you have your own criteria, you can be a success with every run. And then every race can just be a personal best of some description.

Sometimes when you have a fear you don't realise how many people share it. And I'm sure that's what a lot of people with mental health issues are experiencing – suddenly when you're having an open conversation about things, you realise you're not alone. And that was definitely maybe the first thing my aunt, who I used to run with, said every single race we did together. She'd go, 'Oh my God, I hope today's not the day we come last.' So it was a fear. It wasn't enough of a fear to stop me doing what I do, all my races, but it is a fear for many people. And I love that idea that again, no one gets left behind.

Coming last just had this terrible stigma attached to it until it accidentally happened to me. And when I just got so much cheering and I think I got about seven goodie bags because they had leftovers.

And all the staff, the whole marathon, came to cheer me in. It was such a joyous feeling that I then completely lost my fear of coming last.

And now, if I've got a chance of coming second last or last, yes, I will drop back and make sure I'm last cause I like to add to my little tally and it just makes me smile. But I think the thing is, some people feel sorry for you for coming last and I'm always just saying please, save your pity for something worthwhile because I'm so proud of myself that I even started that marathon. I'm actually not losing, I'm achieving, and my tally is going up all the time. It's like a bonus.

I always ask myself, can I take one more step? Because when I want to stop in a race or give up, I say, can you take one more step? And if the answer's yes, I take that step and then I re-evaluate.

I just love the emails that I get, because so many people have just said I've given them permission to enjoy running, which is just obviously cause I enjoy it so much. It's so lovely to have passed that on. And when I started running, it was all about speed and they wouldn't have any people saying it was okay to be slow. And I think there's loads more now, I'm not the only one. And just to have helped people to find their own way to run, and to run on their terms, I think is very, very rewarding. And the funny thing is, half of the people that write to me have then gone on to become really super fast in a very short period of time, or achieve incredible things like run an ultra-marathon within a year of starting running. And I just think, wow, when you give someone permission to do things their way, you never know where they're going to end up and they might end up doing extraordinary things.

My message to would-be runners who feel that they're too old or too unfit or too slow: the first thing I say is running really does welcome everyone. And if you don't believe me, go along to a marathon, go along to any runs and see all the shapes, sizes, ages of people there. And then you'll slowly realise that it is a party where everyone's got an invitation. You don't have to be special to run at all, you just have to want to do it. I know so many people who have the secret ambition to run and I would just say, don't keep it as a secret ambition, just get out there.

The main thing is that I'm not a natural-born runner and the idea that I've chosen something to spend most of my free time doing, which I find incredibly difficult and incredibly challenging, but incredibly rewarding, really excites me. I love upsetting people's expectations of me.

Marathons are always tough for me. I mean, honestly, the bits that click by nicely are very few and far between. I've got lots and lots of things I do. One of them is chanting mantras, like, 'I am fit, I am strong, I will run this marathon.' And then, when I want to make myself laugh, I say, 'I am fit, I am strong, I will look good in my thong.' And I do counting as well. I find counting really soothing and it stops me having panic thoughts about not finishing or having to stop. But my big, big secret weapon is talking, because I just find that sharing my life story and hearing someone else's can make 20 miles go by without me even thinking. I don't actually speak to people before they speak to me. I'm very careful about that. So, I let people approach me and that's why I always wear my battered flamingo hat to every race, because then that breaks the ice – people come over and ask me about it.

The other thing I do is help people that I find struggling. So, I was in danger of not finishing the London Marathon once and I found a woman at the side of the road, sobbing her eyes out, hanging round the neck of her mum. And I just said to her, 'Look, if you give me your daughter, I promise you I'll give her back to you in six hours' time with a medal around her neck. How does that sound?' And the woman said, 'Yeah, take her.' And this woman actually got me through the race that I was in danger of not finishing because I'd been waiting for a long time for someone who didn't turn up, was supposed to meet me at Mile 4. And the baggage buses had already gone by and I was really starting to think I couldn't finish. And she was a faster walker than I was. So actually, in the walking sections, she was the one who kept me focused and in the running sections, I kept her focused. I heard her life story, she heard mine, and we picked up someone else along the way and got her to the finish as well.

So, that day, it started out with tears – I literally was sobbing and I actually thought of just stopping. But I paid a lot for my entry, because I did it for charity, and so I didn't want to disappoint the charity. I had to buy myself a coffee and some biltong, which is dried meat, to cheer myself up. And then after that, I just got the focus back, helping someone else. So I always say to anyone, actually, go and rescue someone else. Because it feels like you get two medals at the end. And she'd read my book. She said to me, 'I know this is a funny thing to say, but have you written a book?' And I went, 'Yeah.' And she said, 'I was reading it last night.' And so, in a rush, she got her boyfriend to go and fetch it, or husband to go and fetch it from the hotel, and he brought it to the finish line and I signed it for him on the finish line.

So, I really would recommend talking, because it makes friends. I've got friends on five continents as a result of running and it's really just an opportunity to connect with people, which I think is very special, and which you don't get in many other sports because you haven't got the time.

MIDNIGHT SUN

Tip: The best training plan is one you can stick to.

There's a scale they use to test hardness, the Mohs scale. Diamonds are 10, talc is 1. If they extended it to marathons, the Midnight Sun would be a 9.

I didn't think it would be. It was meant to be a bit of fun with my brother-in-law, David – a silly weekend in Tromsø as part of his training for an Ironman triathlon. The Midnight Sun Marathon, as the name suggests, is run at midnight in broad daylight. It's not especially hilly and it's all on roads. I thought, on a hardness scale, Tromsø would be a 3 or a 4.

The marathon starts and ends in a picturesque Norwegian port city, deep inside the Arctic Circle. It's the world's northernmost certified marathon. In fact, Tromsø is so far north, the flight up from Oslo takes significantly longer than the flight east to the Norwegian capital from London. In mid-June, it never gets dark. I once spent a year living and working in St Petersburg, where they have an annual White Nights festival. There's something supernatural about midnight daylight, when skies are milky and the sleepy sun never quite retires to bed. I couldn't wait to experience the Norwegian equivalent.

The race begins in Tromsø city centre at 8.30 p.m. on Saturday. The point is to be running, in daylight, as the clock strikes 12. Finishing, ideally, bang on midnight.

I'm a sucker for a themed marathon. These days, there are loads of fun races to choose from and the list is only increasing … Rock 'n' Roll New Orleans, Walt Disney World, Surf City USA, Man vs Horse in Wales, the underground Sondershausen Marathon and the extremely drunken Marathon du Médoc, to name but a few. I'd heard only good things about the Midnight Sun. On a whim one evening, I messaged David to see if he fancied it – how could he not?! – and within an hour, we'd both booked flights.

We didn't exactly think it through. The (expensive) flights meant a total of over 12 hours in the air and less than 20 in Tromsø. Connections were tight both ways, so there was a serious chance we'd either miss the marathon, or work on Monday. We'd also forgotten to book accommodation and by the time we arrived, the only hotel room available in the entire town had a tiny single bed, which we somehow had to share.

But the general folly of the expedition somehow adds to its allure. The quicksilver madness of a midnight sun, everyone out on the streets enjoying the magic way past their bedtime. True *joie de vivre*.

We land into a deluge. There's so much standing water on the tarmac, our feet are drenched on the short walk from the plane to the terminal. The bus to the city centre has to travel at a snail's pace because the driver can barely see where he's going and roads resemble rivers.

It's late afternoon. We register for the race and get another soaking on the way to our hotel. We dry off, only to arrive dripping wet at the pizza place next door. This is rain like we've never seen before.

Having missed lunch, we wolf down three pizzas between us, then head back to change into our kit. At least the marathon will be straightforward. We both want to be running – preferably crossing the finish line – at midnight, which is three and a half hours after the start. We're both in pretty good shape and this shouldn't prove difficult. We agree that the only way we'll have failed is if we finish too early. What's the point in running the Midnight Sun Marathon and completing it before midnight?

The race begins bang on 8.30. It's pleasantly weird to be running past full bars and restaurants. Early on a quiet Sunday morning is our traditional stomping ground. After a quick tour of the town centre, we cross a suspension bridge onto mainland Norway and the route winds along the coastline. All the photos I've seen suggest this is captivating scenery, but the rain remains so heavy, it's hard to see more than a few yards in any direction.

Normally, I love running in the rain – it's a bit like life. As soon as you stop grumbling and resisting it, you can really start to enjoy it. And rain somehow adds to the intensity of a run. Everybody else stays home, so there you are, outside, wet and alone, battling the elements. It makes you feel, well, if not heroic exactly, then certainly gritty. Like you're the sort of person who looks adversity in the eye, raindrops and puddles and all, and says, *give me your best shot*. After all, real life is rarely a perfect, cloudless day.

Running in the rain also reduces stress – the water is cleansing and the sound relaxing. It can even make you run faster and burns more calories by lowering your body temperature. Just remember to put screwed-up newspaper in your shoes afterwards to dry them out.

But here in Tromsø, the rain is different gravy.

The evening is warm and windless, and water is sluicing straight downwards. As we run, we wade through enormous puddles. It feels like being entangled in a soothing dream.

We cross the bridge back into the centre of Tromsø. The bars remain full but the punters have had an extra 90 minutes' drinking time and the encouragement is unquestionably more vocal. And occasionally, a little slurred.

As I pass halfway, I glance at my watch: I've only been going for about an hour and a half. I'm going to have to slow down if I'm not going to finish early.

The second half of the course sees us run to the airport and back. I'm wearing a heavy, long-sleeved running top and keep wringing out the front – it's just so wet. At 15 miles, the road descends to a stony beach and I make an odd decision: I veer off-course and dive fully clothed into the Arctic Ocean.

My reasoning goes something like: I can't get any wetter and I've got time to kill so – why not? Also, I've recently taken to having cold showers and suspect I'll cope admirably with a quick splash in the Arctic. This is the legacy of a meeting with the Dutch extreme athlete Wim Hof, the Iceman. Wim's noted for his ability to withstand freezing temperatures. He's set world records for prolonged immersion in ice and once climbed Mount Everest wearing flip flops. I know he sounds barking – and trust me, I thought the same before I met him – but there's real science behind the madness. Ice turbo charges your immune system and it's kind of addictive once you start.

As soon as the ridiculous notion of a mid-marathon dip enters my soggy brain, I don't hesitate for a moment.

It feels like being stabbed by a million daggers simultaneously. It's cold like I've never even imagined. I'm back out of the water almost as soon as I get in.

I don't regret it immediately. Invigorated by the impromptu ice bath, I power through the next mile in six minutes. One of my fastest miles in any race, and this is Mile 16 of a marathon.

But then … Then come some of the hardest miles of my life.

My whole body begins shaking and feeling very strange. Hard to describe, but what I urgently need to do is lie down somewhere warm and welcoming. Whereas what I'm actually going to do is run another 10 miles in sheet rain.

At this point, my stomach decides to join in the fun: food poisoning. One of those pizzas must've been dodgy. Turns out my brother-in-law has been suffering with this for most of the race, stopping every couple of miles to poo or throw up. I start to do the same.

There's no thought of pulling out, of course. As I may have mentioned, I don't give up during races. If you don't even give yourself the option, it curiously sets you free. But the reading on that Mohs scale of marathon hardness just shot upwards. I'm going to have to guts this one out. Literally.

Bring it on! When the going gets as brutal as this, if we push through, we glimpse who we really are.

There's a 3,100-mile race in New York called the Sri Chinmoy Self-Transcendence Race. It's held annually around the same nondescript block in the New York Borough of Queens. Imagine this: 5,649 identical laps – alongside a freeway, around a High School and past a toddlers' playground. An average of 60-odd miles or 120 laps a day, with normal life going on around you. Competitors have 52 days to complete the distance, running from 6 a.m. to midnight. The prize is typically a tee shirt or a DVD.

Elite endurance athletes sometimes turn up with the idea of smashing the course record. They begin with gusto, gobbling up the miles. But this not a race about glamour and glory, this is stripped-back running with bare needs and basic necessities. After eight or nine days, a strange thing happens: they seem to move beyond ego and slow down. Because the real goal, as the name of the race implies, is self-transcendence. Nine days in, they find it.

The same goes for the monks of Mount Hiei in Japan, who run 1,000 marathons in 1,000 days in search of enlightenment. Dressed in traditional white robes and primitive straw sandals, they clamber up mountains and along precarious paths. A marathon every day for three years. Those who succeed are revered as living saints. In the past 130 years, 46 have managed it.

But on some small level, all of us can glimpse enlightenment when we lace up our running shoes and head outside. Running, especially when it's hard, seems to strip away all the layers and connect you with some primal force within.

We were born to run.

You never commune with nature more profoundly than you do when running in it. And take away our phones, cars and houses, and what are we but part of nature?

There's some beautiful nature around me in Tromsø I'm sure, but all I can see right now is the rain. I'm also lavishly fertilising the local area and grateful that the rain will wash away any trace of it.

The way I mentally carve up a marathon is this. First 10 miles, take it easy and enjoy every moment. Your training has earned you that.

The next six miles are the toughest mentally for me, so I split them into two parkruns. First one to halfway, then a second, slightly shorter parkrun to 16 miles. I'm never allowed to think beyond the next target.

From 16 miles, it's the start of a countdown to the finish: 10, 9, 8, 7, 6 … and each of the last five miles is dedicated to a member of my immediate family. Sometimes I go in descending age order and start with me, but I much prefer to go the other way round and have my own mile last. It's the longest, after all – 1.2 miles from 25 to the finish – and I feel I've earned it.

However, when it's properly difficult, like it is here in Tromsø, then I need to transcend thought. That's when love comes in.

Paula Radcliffe famously repeated the name of her baby daughter Isla on her way to winning the 2008 New York Marathon. She needed to reach beyond her rational brain, her so-called central governor, who was insisting she slow down. So she harnessed pure love.

And love, when all's said and done, is all that's left.

You want proof? Go back to 9/11, that awful day in 2001 when the planes went into the Twin Towers of Manhattan's World Trade Center. What were they all saying down their phones from the hijacked planes and the burning towers when they called to say goodbye? Simply, I love you. Those three words that somehow never cheapen. In the end, there is only love.

Running seems to connect us to the same part of us that feels love. As the marathon monks learn in Japan, beyond thought.

So as the miles tick by and the rain lashes down, I do a Paula and repeat the names of my children, over and over: Emily, Matthew, Mary … Emily, Matthew, Mary … Emily, Matthew, Mary …

Eventually I'm back in the city centre, where by now the locals are decidedly sloshed. Just before I cross the line, I remember to check my watch: it's five to midnight. I've got to keep running for another five minutes, but there's nowhere to go. The finish is no more than 10 yards in front of me. There are barriers and drunk people lining the streets. The only way is backwards.

I pause, dither, then start jogging back towards the airport. This causes general uproar.

'What are you doing!?'

'No, no, get back!'

'Turn around, idiot!'

'You are stupid?'

I'm honestly not doing anyone any harm, but I feel like the car that's broken down on a busy highway. Somebody starts hooting in the traffic jam and now everyone's joining in. The whole of Tromsø seems to be yelling at me.

I don't have much conviction at the best of times, and this is far from the best of times. Not least because I'm utterly desperate for the loo. Obviously, you can't go in the middle of a busy town, especially not when the locals have already taken against you. And I'm properly freezing.

I turn back and sneak over the line three minutes early.

Having caused such a scene by turning back, I feel I need to keep a low profile so I skulk back to the hotel – shame on me – without waiting for Dave to finish. We spend the night taking it in turns to clamber over each other in the cramped single bed to go to the bathroom.

By morning, we're both feeling better and it's still raining. As we land in London, we reflect on our weekend. The journey was expensive, long and stressful. We saw nothing of Tromsø and the surrounding scenery because it was raining so hard. We both got food poisoning, which ruined our races and stopped us sleeping. I went momentarily bonkers and dived into the Arctic Ocean. I didn't even manage to be running the Midnight Sun Marathon at midnight.

Nothing went right. What a truly brilliant weekend. Those Japanese mountain monks have a point, you know. Sometimes marathon running is beyond rational thought.

THE FIRST WOMAN TO RUN AN OFFICIAL MARATHON

'Risk being seen in all your glory.'
Jim Carrey

The word 'inspiration' might have been invented to describe **Kathrine Switzer**. In 1967 she was the first woman to run the Boston Marathon as a registered competitor. They tried to stop her; they failed. Eventually she forced them to change the rules – and she continues to help women worldwide through her 261 Fearless Foundation.

When you've worked on a breakfast show for as long as I have, you learn to guard your sleep very closely. As a consequence, on a day off, there are very few people you'll get up at 4 a.m. for. But when Kathrine said she was free for an afternoon chat (New Zealand-time) just before Christmas, I bounced out of bed in the middle of the night, just as excited as my kids would be a few days later when they ran to discover what Santa had brought.

In 1967 I was a student at Syracuse University. There were no women's sports at all. I had been running on my own and I asked the men's track coach if I could come out and run on the men's team and he said not officially, but he welcomed me to come out and train there. When I came out to train, I was really welcomed by these guys. They were really wonderful. I was really astonished because it was a tough time for the Women's Liberation Movement.

One little volunteer coach in particular, an ex-marathoner who was 50 at the time, he took me under his wing. His name was Arnie Briggs and he would run with me every night. As we increased our mileage, he would tell me stories of the Boston Marathon. It engaged me so much that I told him one night I wanted to run it.

He said, 'A woman can't run the Boston Marathon.'

Women throughout history, there have been about six or seven women who've run marathons, including one in the UK. Anyway, he said, 'If you show me enough in training, I'd be the first person to take you to Boston.' We trained hard and one day we ran 26 miles. I wanted to run further to prove we could go further and finish Boston, and we ran 31 miles, and he passed out at the end of the workout.

He was so convinced then that women had this incredible potential, and endurance, and stamina that he said, 'Okay, let's go. I'll take you to the Boston Marathon. I'm going to honour my promise.'

He said, 'You have to sign up for the race. The other women running didn't wear numbers. That's bad, they really should have worn numbers. You should sign up for the race and pay your entry fee.'

I checked the rule book. There was nothing about gender in the rule book, nothing about gender on the entry form, so we figured it was just a tradition, that there was really going to be nothing wrong. I would be unusual. I'd certainly be noticed, but I was proud of myself, and he was proud of me.

We entered the race and because I signed my name KV Switzer, officials thought the entry was from a man. I signed my name that way because I wanted to be J.D. Salinger, by the way. Anyway, the entry form was accepted, I was issued bib 261, Arnie picked up the bibs for the whole team, we took a group of people there and it was snowing and sleeting. I had on a heavy sweatsuit, looked like one of the guys. I was annoyed about that because I wanted to look good in shorts and a top and show off a little bit because I was very proud of myself. I wasn't there to prove anything, but I was delighted to be a woman and knew I could run this race, it was no problem after the 31-mile workout.

A mile and a half into the race we were all laughing and goofing. The press truck came by us and started taking pictures and going crazy that there was a girl in the race wearing a bib number. And right behind, on the other press truck came Jock Semple, the race director, who was furious that a woman was in his race wearing a bib number. He attacked me and tried to pull off my bib number, screaming, 'Get the hell out of my race and give me those numbers!' He tried to push me off the course.

My coach couldn't get him away from me. He was really out of control. But my boyfriend who was running with me, who was a hulking 235-pound ex All-American football player, hammer thrower guy, threw a crossbody block into the race director and knocked him out of the race instead. Arnie said, 'Run like hell,' and down the street we went.

I was terrified, I was absolutely blindsided by this. I just couldn't understand what was happening. The press truck stayed with us and were very aggressive, yelling at me, 'What are you trying to prove? You don't belong here.' It was very humiliating and very upsetting, but I got very resolute and determined to finish the race, and told Arnie I was going to finish on my hands and my knees if I had to because I knew if I didn't do that, nobody would believe women could run the distance. They would believe women were too weak, and too fragile, and were always barging into places where we weren't welcome. And so I said, 'I'm finishing this race no matter what.'

When I did, I really had come to two conclusions. One, I wanted to become a better athlete because I had a chip on my shoulder. I ran four hours and 20 minutes, and I knew I could do a lot faster than that. And the other one was I wanted to create opportunities for women. The race was a real growing-up experience – I started the race as a girl and ended it as a woman.

I really wanted to change the situation for women. I started by creating running programmes. And then the Olympic Games. I knew that women would run if they had a welcoming, non-intimidating opportunity. And how to create that? I created these dream races in my mind when I was running on long, snowy nights. And I took all these ideas and wrote up a business proposal. I took them to Avon Cosmetics, which at the time was the world's largest cosmetics company.

They loved my ideas and said, 'We might not do anything with running, but why don't you join the company and let's see what happens?' So I did, and I convinced them to do one race. And then they loved the publicity they got from it. It was entirely positive, entirely empowering for women, and they said, 'Let's take up your whole proposal.'

And within five years, we were in 27 countries and five continents. In 1980, we created the Avon International Marathon Championship and closed downtown London for the first time in history for a sports event. Up to that point, the streets had only been closed for the Queen.

There was a lot of lobbying even after that, but in 1981 the then IOC voted the women's marathon into the Olympic Games in 1984, leapfrogging from 3,000 metres right to the marathon. That was huge. To me, it was like giving women the right to vote because it was levelling the physical landscape for us. It was an amazing moment, to go from the Boston Marathon incident to being a broadcaster at the Olympic Games in 1984, and watching those women run incredible times and change attitudes around the world. Two point two billion people watched that event and it changed a lot of minds because everybody in every country knows how far 26 miles, 385 yards or 42.2 kilometres is. They know it's long. It was amazing.

I always say that I'm a meat and potatoes runner, down and dirty, do the work, eat well, try to get some sleep and train hard. I don't believe in magnets and crystals and voodoo-hoodoo and all that stuff. About five or six years ago, suddenly my number from the Boston Marathon in 1967 – 261, which had always just been three digits for 45 years – suddenly became this cult number around the world, meaning fearless in the face of adversity. And what happened is, people were all over the internet seeing the picture of me being attacked in the Boston Marathon and then going on to finish the race. They realised that they really related to that picture because they had also felt sidelined. I mean, we all do. People tell us we can't do something, or we're not worthwhile, or we're too fat, or we're not really an athlete, and then we start running and we feel like we can do anything and we feel fearless. And especially after we do a marathon, we feel we *can* do anything.

People began writing to me and saying, 'This number makes me feel fearless in the face of adversity and I'm wearing your bib on my back tomorrow in the London Marathon,' or whatever. And then they were inking it on their arms, and then they started sending me pictures of their tattoos.

We decided to form a non-profit that reaches out to women everywhere, with an opportunity to put one foot in front of the other and have that same sense of fearlessness that all of us who run feel. And for women running, it's really quite transformational. It's actually beyond running. It's really a social revolution because for thousands of years, women have never had this sense of empowerment and freedom before: running gives it to them.

Have one fearless woman reach out to a fearful woman. Have her come along and start walking or running in a non-judgemental, inviting, companionable way. It's been magic how it's been catching on.

I'm completely excited about women's running because all my life I've devoted myself to it and now we're practically into the second or third generation of kids who are growing up seeing Mommy run and it not being unusual. Our lives are changing and getting healthier. There's a lot more sense of inclusion and equality now.

In North America there are more women runners than there are men. Of all participating runners, 58 per cent are women and the guys don't mind. It's fine. It's one of the greatest stories of inclusion, and diversity, and equality that we have. It illuminates all of us. However, elsewhere there are still huge mental and societal barriers that prevent women from getting into running.

When I go to Southern Spain or parts of South Africa, South America, women are still concerned about losing their femininity and men are still concerned about a woman beating them in a race. In Afghanistan, there are women getting stoned for running. They have to go out and run at two and three in the morning to get their run in when nobody's awake to watch them. It's very, very hard.

But there are breakthroughs. These women are running in groups, they're running in burkas, they're running in their long sleeves and their hijabs. It's breaking through because when they start to feel that freedom, they really want to pass that on and they don't feel a lot of freedom in many other ways because of culture, society, poverty.

Another reason why running is so incredible for women is that it really doesn't take any money and it's totally accessible. You can tell I'm a great believer in what it's doing. We have a long way to go in some societies, but it'll happen. And I think running is a great way to make it happen.

ATHENS CLASSIC

'Your greatest runs are rarely measured by racing success.
They are moments in time when running allows
you to see how wonderful your life is.'
Kara Goucher, US distance runner,
World Championship silver medallist

If running is your thing, then you can't *not* run the Athens Classic Marathon. It's the route that began it all 2,500 years ago. And it's the route that brought it back to life in 1896.

You may remember the ancient Greek messenger Pheidippides rushing home to Athens with urgent news of a phenomenal victory in battle (see also page xiv). He ran from Marathon to Athens in 490BC. He was alone. Today there are thousands of us all running the same path.

We've just left Marathon, heading for the Panathenaic Stadium in Athens, venue for the first modern Olympics. Baron Pierre de Coubertin founded those Games in 1896 and made the marathon their centrepiece. This lavishly moustachioed Frenchman wanted athletes to mirror his philosophical ideal, valuing competition for its own sake. Hence his famous quote: 'The important thing in life is not the triumph but the struggle. The essential thing is not to have conquered but to have fought well.'

Little-known fact, de Coubertin actually won an Olympic gold medal himself, at the Stockholm Games of 1912, when literature was included in the programme for the one and only time. He wowed the judges with his poem, *Ode to Sport*.

As for the marathon, initially the distance was set at 40 km or 24.85 miles. It was lengthened for the 1908 London Olympics so the runners could run the 26 miles from Windsor Castle to the White City Stadium, followed by a 385-yard lap of the track to finish in front of the Royal Box. And bizarrely, when they decided to set the official distance in 1924, that's the one they chose. From then on, a marathon has been exactly 26.22 miles or 42.195 km. And the legacy of Baron Pierre – and Pheidippides before him – is celebrated by the massed ranks of hopefuls who take on the iconic distance all over the world, every weekend of the year.

Especially here, especially this weekend. We're recreating Pheidippides' run and following in the footsteps of those early Olympians. Albeit with a tad more tarmac, Lycra and much better GPS.

You start in Marathon by raising your right hand and solemnly proclaiming a slightly bastardised version of the Olympic Oath. Something like, '*We promise that we shall take part in this race, respecting and abiding by the rules which govern it, committing ourselves to sport without doping or drugs, in the true spirit of sportsmanship, for the glory of sport and the honour of our nations.*' Thousands of nervous, excited runners reciting that before embarking on the race that began it all – it's spine-tingling stuff.

The road from Marathon to Athens is unremarkable, and mostly uphill. There's a 10-km section where you never stop climbing. However the locals appreciate the fact that you're honouring their history and culture by taking part – which of course you absolutely are – so they turn out in their numbers to thank you and cheer you on. You finish in the all-marble Panathenaic Stadium, feeling like an Olympian of old. The whole atmosphere, every bit of this race, is very special.

I've been desperate to run Athens ever since I finished my first marathon in Barcelona a decade ago. Eleven minutes in, just outside Marathon, I change my mind and turn back to the start.

I've ducked under the barriers onto the opposite side of the road but my decision – and direction of travel – causes much consternation among fellow runners. I don't want to put people off their stride, so I change my mind again and clamber onto a roadside bollard. I'm trying to pick out one runner in particular.

Two years previously, Nick Butter came up with the idea of running a marathon in every country of the world. I first interviewed him about it when he started in Barbados. We met in person just before the London Marathon when he told me he was planning to finish his personal odyssey where it all started for the marathon, in Athens. I was coming anyway with some pals from Barnes Runners, so Nick and I hatched a vague plan to run this together.

On the start line, I discovered Nick had a triumphant entourage with him and would run at the pace of the slowest of them. He would also start at the back of the field so his moped-riding cameraman wouldn't get in everybody's way. They were filming the entire journey for a documentary, *Running the World 196*.

To be honest, I baulked at the idea of taking 20 minutes to cross the start line and a further five hours to reach the finish. So I made an excuse and scampered back to the front with running club pals, Sam, Chris and Richard. Besides, we were flying home that same evening so needed to finish running early enough to enjoy a few well-earned local beers in the shadow of the Acropolis. A five-hour marathon would severely dent those celebrations.

It rained briefly but hard soon after we started running. The mood I was in, I took this as an omen. Because the previous week, messing about as we do on the breakfast show where I work, we'd all taken our blood pressures. Mine was through the roof. I laughed it off, but none of the usual causes applied to me so I admit to being concerned.

Under the circumstances, an overnight jaunt to Greece to run 26.2 miles seemed somewhat irresponsible for a doting husband and father of three. After lengthy discussions with my wife Caroline, we decided to leave it to our local GP to decide if I should run, but we weren't able to arrange an appointment in time. They only had emergency appointments available and I could just imagine the response if I'd taken one of those. *Doctor, it's an emergency, I've got to run a marathon!* I'm not sure running a marathon has ever counted as an emergency since Pheidippides.

So the plan is to take it easy. Which I'm demonstrably ignoring as I pass two miles in just over 13 minutes. The rain brings me to my senses.

The course turns left down a side road, loops around an ancient monument, returns to the main highway and continues onwards to Athens. This is where I decide instead to turn back towards Marathon in search of Nick, dither, then climb a bollard to look out for him.

A woman dressed as a giant vegetable sees me and stops to chat. She's also looking for Nick, who's been a big inspiration to her as she completes her own challenge: a marathon on each continent dressed as a different fruit or veg. She was – naturally – a big apple in New York a fortnight ago, and today she's an aubergine. Together, we find Nick and his team.

Throughout the challenge, Nick's been raising money for Prostate Cancer UK. He shared a tent with a man called Kevin Webber during a race in the Sahara and was inspired by his determination and resilience in the face of a terminal cancer diagnosis. According to that diagnosis, Kevin should be long dead by now. But here he is, cheerfully keeping pace with Nick's entourage on the suburban streets of Greece. The others have all been touched or inspired by the story and want to join the victory lap. One of them met Nick in Serbia and quit his job to help organise the dizzying logistics, including booking 400 flights, all of which I'm pleased to learn had the carbon offset.

Nick has run marathons in 196 countries, in 60-degree heat and in cold of minus 25. He's been bitten, mugged, put in a cell and hit by a car. As we run gently towards Athens, I ask him why he did it and what he's learned.

If I'm lucky enough to get to the point in life when I'm old and grey, chatting with my grandchildren, I want to know I've explored every inch of the planet. I want to have exhausted every ounce of my potential, challenged myself beyond what is comprehensible and know I did everything in my power to make the best use of my time; to love, to work hard, and to spend as little time as possible in the so-called comfort zone.

I believe that it's the crazy things, the things that no one is doing, and the things that we're afraid to do which are exactly what leave a positive mark on the world. I want to leave the world better than I found it. By exploring, being appreciative, pushing myself to my limits, and never sitting back and saying I've finished.

My achievement will hopefully inspire young minds, old minds, any minds, that we can all do our bit to value the time we have on this wonderful planet. Even if our bit is just being grateful for today. Tomorrow is a maybe, today is a privilege, let's go make the most of today.

I'm surrounded by beaming faces. Joy sparkles all around and the euphoria makes us giddy. We stop for photos, interviews, and always move at the pace of the slowest runner. This is not a race to Athens, this is a celebration. Almost the exact opposite of Pheidippides' original dash along this same route 2,500 years ago. He needed to deliver the message from the battlefield as quickly as possible. We'll simply arrive when we arrive and make the most of every mile along the way. We feel no need, no need for speed.

It's a revelation to me, running a marathon like this. Or rather, jogging a marathon like this. Often walking. When I'm asked to give talks before races, I frequently advise anyone listening: 'Don't let your time ruin your time.' I use the quote, but largely ignore it when it comes to my own races. Today, for the first time ever in a marathon, I don't even glance at my watch. With a few miles to go, I run on ahead. I want to leave Nick to enjoy this final finish line with Kevin and the team. Besides, there are beers to be drunk with fellow Barnes Runners. And frankly, at this rate I may have to rush straight from the 1896 Stadium to the brand-new airport built for the latest Greek Games of 2004.

Nick's big finish will be every bit as monumental as the occasion deserves. The following day, he's on every news outlet and in every newspaper. He now plans to inspire a new generation to run, explore and understand different cultures. He collected a memento from every country in the world and takes them all with him when he does talks in schools. One of the good guys. A real inspiration to me and now to thousands of others.

It's difficult to find my stride after pottering along for so long. I'm among runners aiming for sub-five hours rather than my usual three-hour brigade. They say it's still a well-run marathon if it's under five hours – a proper marathon. I tend to disagree. A marathon finished is a marathon won regardless of how long it takes.

I discover that this is the place in the field where people chat, make friends and encourage each other. Yet I find I'm more in the mood for sober reflection. The blood pressure thing. When I arrive home and check, it's totally fine. The doctor suspects a rogue reading or a faulty machine. But I don't know that in Athens and as ever, running gives me the perspective I need.

I continue to go slowly, keeping the heart rate nice and low. Also, the one time I speed up to my normal race pace and begin streaking past runner after runner, I feel a little silly. So I plod onwards, determined to be grateful for the moment.

It's hard *not* to be grateful when you arrive in Athens and finish in that magnificent marble stadium. Even more so, an hour later, when you catch up with your mates and realise the great Ron Hill is on the table next door and he joins you for a beer.

Ron once won the Athens Marathon, one of many stellar achievements in a fantastic career. He set world records at four different distances, was the second man in history to break 2:10 for the marathon, won numerous gold medals. He founded Ronhill clothing. And he famously owns the world's longest run streak, running every day for 52 years and 39 days. From 1964 to 2017, he ran at least a mile every single day – even after breaking his sternum in a car crash, even after bunion surgery, which left him on crutches.

If we could've chosen anyone in the world to share a beer with after running the marathon which began it all, it would've been Ron Hill. Just epic.

THE BLIND MARATHON RUNNER WHO FELL IN LOVE WITH HIS GUIDE

'Never confuse a single defeat with a final defeat.'
F. Scott Fitzgerald

Anthony Butler is a visually impaired runner from New York. **Jessie Rix** is his guide. They fell in love while running marathons tethered together. They've completed races as far afield as Chicago and Paris. Jessie guides Anthony's feet, fills in the necessary blanks, paints the pictures – *High curb to the right! Louvre on your left!*

ANTHONY

I grew up in the Bronx in Harlem. I did grow up with both parents but there was lots of instability in the household and just all kinds of drama. It was a very unstable household and I just grew up with lots of trauma. In 2008, I was 20 years old, I was a victim of a shooting, which resulted in the loss of my vision. I gained a lot of weight, probably 50–60 pounds after I was shot. I was just trying to work out but my friends, they just weren't really into it. There's no working out when you're staying up all night.

We probably would drink some beers and then I would go to the 24-hour gym at 5:00 in the morning – probably did that once every week or two.

I was like, 'This isn't really doing it for me.' Everybody was still into smoking and selling drugs, and I wasn't able to do that anymore. I wasn't into it. I was going back to school and I was trying to get on the right track.

I didn't really have any other friends that were blind and I was needing a community of my own so I was talking to my social worker about options and she was like, 'There's a group out there called Achilles International, which aims to empower people with all types of disabilities to participate in mainstream running events.' And she called, and she told me to show up, and she signed me up and they sent me a shirt. And I went to a workout, and that was six, seven years ago, and I've been going ever since.

JESSIE

I'm originally from Minnesota and I moved to New York in 2012. And I've been a runner basically my whole life. It's something I think I started in about the fifth grade. It was something I was good at and it became kind of a therapy for me. I was running cross country and track and all that stuff.

So I just continued. Once I got to New York, I really didn't have a team or companionship to have people that I ran with. A lot of my friends didn't run and it would take a lot of my social life away because I'd be training for something or I'd want to go for a run in the morning, and that wasn't fitting what they were looking to do. So I ran in Central Park a lot and I saw Achilles. They wore these bright neon yellow shirts in the park and I saw them and I was like, 'You know what, maybe I need to like, jump in and see what this is about.'

So I kind of just joined one day and started talking to a few people there. The first day I came, I saw Anthony and I mean, he was just super full of life and talking and laughing. He had tonnes of people around him and I was like, 'Okay, he just looks like a fun person to run with.' And that's exactly what I was looking for, some running friends that I could spend my social time with as well on top of running and not have to make time for the both of it. I could just kind of bring those worlds together. So, I kind of hopped on with Anthony's group and I ran with Anthony and two of his friends. And after that, I just kind of kept coming back until here we are today.

ANTHONY

As a blind runner, for me personally, I'm a real easy-going person so I always try to make the other person feel comfortable. I try to show them that this is really not about me. Sure, they're helping me meet my goals, but if they're not comfortable, we're not really going to have a good race. So I make sure that their stride is correct. I tell them to be as natural as possible because I need them to be comfortable with it.

If they're thinking too much then we're probably going to trip or just go down so I try to make sure that they're at ease with that. But, it's fun, you know what I mean? It gives me a sense of a community. I've run marathons all over the place. And anytime you're able to go somewhere else that's not full of sirens and noise and people just being so loud and aggressive, it just makes you feel good. And just reminds me how lucky I am to be here and to get a second chance at life.

JESSIE

I don't know if I was naturally suited to guide running. It's been a learning process and even still is a learning process. I quickly learned how every individual is different, they have different needs, and being able to communicate and voice that with them. I'm naturally more of an introverted person so even jumping into Achilles, that was a big step for me. That's not something I would naturally do. But whether I'm guiding Anthony or somebody else, it's knowing that each person has different needs and they have different goals, and it's how to accommodate those but still have a great time.

When Anthony and I travel, I'm just voicing everything I'm seeing around me so he can be a part of it. Anything that I'm seeing, even if it's someone wearing something silly on the course, I'll describe it to Anthony, because I want him to share that memory with me. As long as he's there, even if he doesn't see it, that's all that matters.

So, it's been a few years so I've gotten a lot better at it, I hope. It can be stressful. We have a great time but we've definitely had those stressful runs too. It can be very difficult watching everything and being in the middle of a race with tonnes of runners around and a new terrain and a new country and a new language, so kind of figuring out how to navigate all those things, but still come out on top and have a great time. So it's definitely a learning process, but it's worth every second.

ANTHONY

I think Chicago was my favourite race. I was feeling good. I probably ran the first 15-16 miles straight, no breaks. But it was really hot and so I started to struggle a bit. But I was like, 'You know what? I'm not going to hit my goal time,' because I was trying to qualify for Boston. So we decided – let's just have some fun. And we just danced the rest of the way, we took Jello shots, we drank beer, we hopped off people and we just had a good time. We finished the race, but we just made it fun. We just had a good time.

JESSIE

I agree, I agree 100 per cent. Honestly, it was a very hot day and I remember I was joking about how we can't get a regular-weathered marathon that year because every marathon we ran was at least 80 degrees. So, Anthony did a phenomenal job and the fact that he ran like 16–17 miles nonstop, that was a huge goal. A huge accomplishment. So that was awesome. And I remember at one point he just got so hot and he's like, 'Oh, I just need some ice.' And some random stranger was like, 'Oh, I got ice.' It was almost like a sign from God. We're like, 'All right, we're going to make it through this. We're going to get there.' But like Anthony said, we just had the best time. Every time there was a good song that was blaring over the loudspeakers, we would just stop and dance and we would take photos together. It genuinely was such a fun time.

And once you finish Chicago, they have a beer waiting for you right at the end, before you even get your medal. So we finished. We were hot, we were tired, but we felt awesome. And I don't really remember any lows of that race just because we just made it into the best time. And no matter what, the pain you go through, you always remember the good times over the bad, right?

BACCHUS

'A good laugh and a long run are the two best cures for anything.'
Unknown

A group of 20 or so runners in a *Help the Aged* minibus arrive in the car park of an English vineyard. The mood is sombre, which is unusual at the start of any marathon, let alone one which encourages fancy dress and offers wine and champagne at the aid stations.

This is the Bacchus Marathon, an annual colourful, hilly, boozy, athletic carnival.

It begins in the picturesque Denbies Vineyard nestled at the bottom of Box Hill in an official 'Area of Outstanding Natural Beauty'. It ends there too, with a raucous party. The glorious Surrey hills link the Kent Downs to the east with the South Downs to the south-west. On a shiny September morning like this, there are few finer places.

It's still early as we climb out of the rented bus. Almost 2,000 runners will soon descend on this little corner of England, but few have arrived before our motley gang. The air is fresh, the sky California blue, the surrounding hills radiant green. Birdsong all around. The swifts and swallows seem to be circling for the simple pleasure of flight, dancing.

This has long been a popular event among members of Barnes Runners and never have more of us turned up to run it. But our mood remains melancholy.

A few months ago, we lost a good friend and club member. Liam Whelan was in many ways the lifeblood of our little running club, rarely missing a Tuesday evening 10k – and never missing a few pints in the Coach and Horses afterwards. He was also a committed marathon runner. Most weekends, you'd find him trundling round 26.2 miles somewhere or other, as he edged ever closer to the coveted 100 Marathon Club vest. He'd run 91 when he died suddenly, shockingly, of heart failure, one Saturday evening. His 100th was due to be today, at the irreverent Bacchus, his absolute favourite race.

Which is why none of us is in fancy dress today. We're all wearing our white, blue and green club colours with a black ribbon pinned to the front. This race, for us, is in memory of our friend. We drink tea and chat distractedly.

I'm also thinking about the young man I met in Manchester, the chef I spoke to briefly on his way to a PB. He didn't mention it as we run through suburbs, but I later discovered he'd reached the semifinals of *MasterChef*. I heard it on the news when, tragically, Matt Campbell lost his life, a fortnight later. Matt collapsed 22.5 miles into the hottest London Marathon on record and later died in hospital. The following Sunday, thousands congregated where he fell to 'Finish for Matt', raising half a million pounds for the charity he was supporting. He was running in honour of his father Martin, who'd worked for the Brathay Trust.

Matt's death was heartbreaking and sad to say, very occasionally, people do die during marathons. However, in almost all cases, it's not the running that's to blame, or even the distance. Time and again, running has been proven to reduce your risk of dying prematurely. But everybody dies, and some die while running. A study by the American College of Cardiology found that the risk of death from running a marathon is 0.8 per 100,000 people, which is significantly lower than dying during childbirth in the UK (8.6 in 100,000 births).

Professor Greg Whyte is an Olympian-turned-sports physiology professor. It was Greg's know-how which helped comedian Eddie Izzard complete his spectacular 43 marathons in 51 days for Comic Relief in 2009:

> Of course it makes headlines when somebody dies during a big city marathon, but there's always a reason. Unless you have pre-existing underlying cardiovascular disease, running is very positive and will improve the health of your heart.

It was a pre-existing heart problem that did for our friend Liam.

We gather on the start line a minute before the off. We turn to each other, almost surprised to find ourselves on the brink of running a marathon. These things are never easy, and especially not with the added Surrey Hills, but the fact of our impending physical exertions seems not to have occurred to any of us. It's all very weird.

Then the gun goes and we're running.

Liam was in his mid-50s when he died. He was an excellent runner when the mood took him, annually qualifying for a Good for Age place in the London Marathon and a sub-20 minute parkrunner. But for the majority of his many marathons, he'd take it easy and jog home in around three and a half hours, sometimes four. (I know, of course, that 3:30 to 4 hours is a relatively quick marathon time, and significantly faster than the UK average of 4:37:09, but for an experienced and rapid runner like Liam, it represents quite an easy effort.)

While several club-mates tear off at the front, I follow Liam's lead and run within myself. It's my first time running the Bacchus and the hilliness surprises me. The hilliness and also the silliness: very few runners are not in fancy dress.

The race is the brainchild of local running-shop owner Alan Burrows. He got the idea from the Marathon du Médoc in Bordeaux, which at first glance seems like the most idiotic race on Planet Earth: 26.2 miles in compulsory fancy dress, with 23 wine stops also offering oysters, foie gras, cheese, steak and ice cream. Yet 10,000 runners from 50 different countries make the annual pilgrimage and return home with happy hangovers. Alan lived next door to the biggest vineyard in the UK, and one day the head of the Denbies events team walked into his shop to buy trainers. Within 24 hours they'd hatched a plan, somehow persuaded the local council to get on board and the Bacchus was born.

The previous year, Liam had sat in the sunshine with fellow Barnes Runners after the race, enjoying a beer or two. Music was playing, the party was in full swing. Full of endorphins – and alcohol – Liam declared emphatically that he must've died and gone to heaven. The heartbreaking irony that, 12 months on, he'd done exactly that is lost on none of us – and on the day he was due to celebrate entry to the 100 Marathon Club too. We may not be in fancy dress, but we're definitely here to celebrate life. During the race, I'm sure I'm not alone in frequently reaching to touch the black ribbon pinned to my club vest.

We run through the vineyards on the lower slopes of Box Hill and the miles seem to fly by. The views are sumptuous, England's green and pleasant land at its finest. Four miles in gives us the first chance to sample the local tipple being grown all around. On wide grassy paths among acres of lush-looking vines, smiling volunteers stand behind fold-up tables on which they've laid dozens of little beakers of chilled white wine. There's also water on offer, but in this sunshine the wine won't stay chilled for long. Almost rude not to have a try. *Go on then, just a little.* Goes down surprisingly easily.

The course dives into the trees and heads steeply upwards. Box Hill is where they held the Olympic cycling road races in 2012. It's not exactly the Matterhorn, but in south-east England, it's the best we've got and a mecca for weekend cyclists. They flock here in their hundreds and in their Lycra every Saturday and Sunday morning, reaching the summit via the wonderfully named Zig Zag Road. As we runners climb through the woods, I keep expecting us to emerge into a sea of Sunday cyclists – until I realise we're the other side of the valley.

Not that the views are anything less than spectacular west of the River Mole. We climb through the trees onto a stunning slope with the Surrey Hills laid bare below us, then descend into woods once more.

Every few miles, happy volunteers offer us booze. Having just tripped on a root and almost head-butted a tree, I decide to quit while I'm even vaguely ahead and mostly opt for water.

Another steep climb past a picturesque church and we find ourselves running around the manor house at the top of the vineyard and into an aid station with English sparkling wine on offer. I was once given a bottle of this as a thank you by the Rugby Football League. I'm embarrassed to say I inwardly scoffed when I saw it, thinking it was poor person's champagne. Turns out I couldn't have been more wrong. First, it's more expensive than many champagnes. And more to the point, it's absolutely delicious.

So yes, I have some. Toast Liam. *Only a mile to go*, says the man passing over a second glass, *and it's all downhill.*

Which is absolutely spot on. One gentle, easy, downhill mile to go … for everyone running the half-marathon. I remember the fact that I have another full circuit still to go, another 14 miles, just as I hand back the empty glass. Oh well.

At the bottom of the glorious hill with the welcoming finish line in front of me, I won't pretend it wasn't tempting not to carry on and just accept a half-marathon medal. This is a perennial temptation in all marathons that are simply two laps of the half course. It was slightly more tempting than usual with a bit of booze inside me. But dutifully I found myself turning left and setting off on another 13-mile lap.

And honestly, the second lap was sensational. It reinforced how much I'd enjoyed the first. I sensibly refused all alcohol from then on – until the sparkling wine near the finish.

Others were not so abstemious. I passed several half-marathon groups who'd set off later and were enjoying themselves royally. You do feel a little conspicuous in a running club vest, chasing up behind a walking, giggling group containing Wonder Woman, Elvis and some Smurfs and asking them to step to the side of the path so you can come crashing through. They basically laugh at you – *ooh, real runner alert!* – and rightly so.

On the way back down the hill I have a moment of melancholy. It's impossibly sad not to have Liam with us today, not to be celebrating the achievement he spent years pursuing. It seems like such a waste, to be denied by a dodgy heart with nine marathons to go.

As I jog down the gentle hill to the finish, an old cartoon springs to mind, one I saw in the in-flight magazine on the way to Barcelona for my first marathon. Best pals Snoopy and Charlie Brown looking out to sea:

'We only live once, Snoopy.'
'Wrong! We only die once. We live every day.'

Liam, with his humour, zest for life and mild marathon addiction, crammed far more into his short years than most could ever hope to. And he'd have been proud of the party we held in his honour all afternoon. And evening.

THE MAN WITH THE LONGEST QUEST TO BREAK THREE HOURS

Tip: Over 40? Add some weight/resistance training to your running routine to compensate for your body's natural decline in muscle mass.

David Cornock is a BBC political correspondent and presenter, and a good pal. It's his fault I joined Barnes Runners, so his fault I flog myself round Richmond Park every Tuesday evening – and often his fault I stay for one too many in the pub afterwards. He ran his first marathon soon after his 18th birthday, and finally broke the magic three-hour barrier a few days after he turned 50. So, just your fifth decade of trying then, Dave!

The Cardiff Marathon used to go past our front door. That inspired me to start running. So at the age of 18, just after I'd done my A-levels, I started training for it. I didn't have anything as vulgar as a watch, no GPS of course. It took me 3:48, which I only found out when the *Western Mail* published the results on the following Wednesday. But it's a day you never forget. And even if that'd been my only one, it was an incredibly special day running through our village, seeing friends and neighbours.

It was only in my 40s that I realised I'd been jogging all along – and if I'd realised how hard it was to break three hours, I'd probably have put a bit more effort in sooner. When we moved to Barnes, very leafy, perfect running country, I started getting dedicated, if not obsessed. I got down to 3:09.

Before each marathon I used to get absolutely paranoid, complete maranoia. I was once so nervous before London, I offered to send the rest of the family away for the weekend. Then I won some coaching with supercoach Martin Yelling and he sent through this question-naire. First question is, what would your dream marathon time be? Well, ask a stupid question. So, I put 2:59:59 and Martin devised this schedule and I started doing intervals.

I ran 3:07 and I ran 3:05. Like my O-level results, I can still remember all my marathon times down to the second. It's slightly embar-rassing. When you're on the cusp of that three hours, it's like a batsman who knows he's going to be out for 99 every time, or 101. There isn't a lot to play with. It's ridiculous for a middle-aged recre-ational runner and actually quite stressful. I think if I put as much effort into the rest of my life as I had into breaking three hours, then I'd have been Husband of the Year, Father of the Year and prime minister. But hey, I've got a sub-three marathon.

London 2013, I ran three hours and 58 seconds. It took me a few weeks to get over that. Then I booked Amsterdam for later that year, two days into my fifties. I'd had injuries in the run-up. I'd had physio. I'd had a pelvic problem. And because of the injuries, I was a bit worried I wasn't going to make it round. But it was booked, so I went – but I put an Amsterdam travel card in the back pocket of my shorts just in case.

I started at sub-3 pace, around 6 minutes 45 per mile. Although I've never been the fastest runner, I'm quite good at pacing and dialling into a pace and keeping it. I was hitting the target so it was going well, but I had this nagging doubt that I wouldn't be able to finish because I've had all these problems. Then I had to have a pit stop at 30 kilometres.

I had developed a little bit of a stomach problem. Probably had a gel too early or too much breakfast. So luckily, there was a portaloo and I did a sort of Lewis Hamilton-style pit stop – in at 45 degrees, out at 45 degrees. Check the data after. It took 52 seconds, which is probably a PB in itself.

And then I kept going. And it was when I got to 40k, coming back through the park, there's 2k to go and I remember thinking there's still 10 minutes to go, this is on. I'm thinking, just keep going. Martin Yelling told me control, effort, mindset. Just keep focused, tick along, smile when someone says your name, another little trick.

And it was just outside the stadium, 500 metres to go, crossing the tramlines, and I suddenly thought, Wow, I'm going to do this! You can see the surprise on my face in the finishing photos. And I didn't want to smash three hours, I wanted it to be 59. I mean, it would have been 58 but for my pit stop – but just perfect. It was perfect. There's quite a few of my running PBs have a 9 in them, which illustrates sufficient effort, but not excessive.

I think people who break three hours react in two ways. One you say, 'Well, what's all the fuss about it? It wasn't too difficult, was it?' And there's the other where you think as time goes by, God, how did I do that? And when I belt round my local parkrun and I can't even hit my marathon pace, 21 minutes for 5k, and I think only a few years ago, I ran eight and a half of those back-to-back at that pace. And I realise, yeah, it was worth doing.

It means a lot more when you're older. I did it two days after my 50th birthday, two days after I became eligible to go to Age UK yoga and book a Saga holiday.

I then played around with these age calculators you can find and realised it would have been so much easier if I'd done it in my 20s or my 30s, because it was the equivalent of about 2:37. It would've been so much simpler just to do it younger. But less rewarding. I promptly retired from road marathons but still enjoy racing.

And the only time I go to that age calculator now is when I've got club-mates in their 40s like you, who think you're faster than me.

You don't know just how difficult it gets.

NEW YORK CITY

Tip: When you cross the finish line, however knackered you are, keep moving as a courtesy to other runners.

'All happy families are alike; every unhappy family is unhappy in its own way.' So writes Leo Tolstoy, in the opening words of *Anna Karenina*. The same is largely true of marathons. When they're going well, the miles just seem to tick by smoothly, serenely, almost effortlessly. But woe betide you when a marathon goes pear-shaped.

And no marathon has ever gone south sooner, spiralled into meltdown earlier, than my maiden attempt to conquer New York.

Any chance of a good race essentially evaporated at 5 a.m. on Race Day as I sprinted around the streets of Manhattan in a mounting sense of panic. Even as I marvelled at how easy sprinting seemed on my freshly tapered legs, I knew the morning was unlikely to end in one of those smooth, straightforward races. Not when I also thought I could be shot any second by an increasingly irate US state trooper …

Let's leave me for a moment about to be arrested in the pre-dawn and rewind 36 hours. We'd landed in New York on

Friday evening, myself and seven wonderful charity auction winners, who raised loads of money for BBC Children in Need. I was helping deliver a special package, including a training run with Paula Radcliffe and VIP entry into the London and New York City marathons.

London couldn't have gone better and New York was shaping up to be equally wonderful. We'd enjoyed a convivial dinner soon after arriving (by stretch limo, no less!), then on Saturday morning, a leisurely jog around Central Park with the legendary Paula, serial champion in New York and long-time marathon world record holder. She's fantastically popular in the Big Apple – as we ran, we were pleasantly mobbed by excitable locals eager for selfies. Paula even steered us back on track when we got a little lost in the park, before returning us safely to the sidewalk on Sixth Avenue opposite the official race hotel, where we were lucky enough to be staying.

'The courtesy bus will pick you up right here at 5:15 tomorrow morning,' Paula helpfully informed us.

Now under normal circumstances, I'd have been sure to double check. Any journalist worth their salt will tell you it's vital to verify a fact with a second credible source. Very occasionally, you go to air with a single source – but only when that source is the definition of unimpeachable. Which, on matters pertaining to the marathon, Paula Radcliffe unquestionably is. Especially the New York Marathon, which she won three times out of three.

So when Paula told us the bus would be waiting on Sixth Avenue, opposite the Hilton, I took it as gospel and arranged to meet the other runners, our auction winners, at 5 a.m. in the lobby.

I hadn't counted on two things. First, the lifts. Who knew that it can take 10 minutes to get to the ground floor when every other guest in the 33-storey hotel is also running the marathon and fervently pressing the down button? This made us all a little late, which would have been fine – except that Paula was only half-right about the bus.

It does indeed leave at 5:15 from Sixth Avenue opposite the Hilton Hotel – *but only if you're one of the elite women*. The bus we needed, for invited guests of New York Road Runners, was nowhere to be seen. I knew it would be departing any second, but had no clue where from. There was doubtless a relevant email on my phone which would tell me exactly where to find the bus. But the phone was in my room, two 10-minute journeys away in the bloody hotel lifts.

Which is why I could be found sprinting in ever-increasing circles around the shadowy streets of Manhattan, terrified we'd miss the bus. With the streets closed and the ferries all booked up, there was no other way to reach Staten Island. We we were in grave danger of failing to accomplish what we'd flown 3,500 miles – and our auction winners had paid many thousands of pounds – to do, namely run the New York City Marathon.

With seconds to spare, I spot the last of the correct buses about to depart from Times Square. I stand on the bottom step near the driver, one foot squarely inside the bus and the other on the sidewalk. I scream for the others to hurry up and join me. The driver is becoming antsy, urging me to decide one way or another, in or out, stop blocking the door – he's *gotta move on outta here.*

This being New York, there are police outriders ready to escort the bus across town. Sensing the commotion, an armed policeman (they're all armed, we're in America after all) struts over to investigate. He advises me, in that calm, ominous manner of a man with a gun, to *step away from the vehicle.*

It's still dark outside. The wide avenues of Manhattan are eerily quiet, bereft of traffic. Steam erupts from the roadside vents.

'Sir, I'm going to ask you again. Step. Away. From the vehicle.'

Of course, he never comes close to reaching for that gun of his, but it's all I can think about. Should I do as I'm told and miss the last bus to the start, or stay where I am and risk taking a bullet for the team?

Imagine Hugh Grant in any of those early rom-coms, eyelids desperately fluttering, nervously stammering in that cut-glass accent of his. That's me as I attempt a curious cocktail of British charm and blind panic in a bid to buy some time.

One by one, painstakingly slowly, the runners in our party hear my shouts and find the bus. Eventually, just as the policeman looks over my shoulder and tells the driver to just close the door and leave, the last of our runners shows up and we climb on board a moving bus. Shaking with mingled fear, relief and embarrassment, we stumble to our seats under the withering looks of the other, impatient passengers.

Mind you, I don't know what their hurry was.

The journey to Staten Island takes about an hour. That leaves a minimum of three hours to hang around before the mass start. I say a minimum of three, because it's such a big race, they start you in waves according to your projected finish time. I was lucky – having run London in 2:59, I was at the front of Wave 1. Other members of our party had another two hours before Wave 4 set off. That's five hours' expending nervous energy in the chill of a New York November morning – without getting so much as a millimetre closer to the finish line in Central Park. There are also stringent, airport-style security checks and the stress of finding your way to the right starting pen, or 'corral' in local speak.

This is the world's biggest marathon – over 50,000 will cross the finish line today – and the hullabaloo before the start reinforces that fact. It must be a logistical nightmare.

Runners line up on both levels of the massive Verrazzano-Narrows Bridge, which links Staten Island and Brooklyn. Back in the day, those on the bottom level spent the minutes before the start dodging streams of urine as runners above them emptied their bladders over the sides of the bridge. I'm relieved to see no evidence of this happening today – indeed there are signs warning of dire consequences should anyone so much as *think* of weeing in public.

Even so I'm thrilled to be on the top level, just in case. The thought of having to run a marathon drenched in wee! A GB ultra-runner once told me how she popped into a portaloo 16 hours into a 24-hour endurance race round a running track. In the pitch-dark, she used her hands to ease herself onto the loo seat – as you would if you'd been running 16 hours straight – only to find that the previous occupant had missed the toilet so she'd just placed her hand in a small mound of human faeces. She spent the final eight hours of the race – eight hours! – wearing someone else's poo as a glove.

Like I say, I'm thankful to be on the top level of the bridge.

I'll tell you what, though, the start of the New York City Marathon is really awesome. There are speeches, hands placed on hearts for the national anthem. Then all of a sudden, after months of training and hours of build-up, you're away and running across the start line to the unmistakable, inspiring strains of Frank Sinatra's rendition of 'New York, New York'. You glance around you and exchange smiles … this is what it's all about.

The first mile is all uphill, the second entirely downhill; two halves of the longest suspension bridge in the Americas. After that, you're on a journey through the boroughs of New York and each one has its own distinct character.

First, Brooklyn. Well, first was Staten Island where the race starts, but you're not there for long. Or rather, not running there for long. The route then winds along Fourth and Bedford Avenues through evocative-sounding neighbourhoods like Bay Ridge, Sunset Park, Bedford-Stuyvesant, Williamsburg and Greenpoint. Those last two have large Jewish populations and it's not unusual to see a rabbi crossing the race route as if nothing abnormal is happening – *I normally cross Fourth Avenue at this time on a Sunday, so that's exactly what I'm going to do today.'* Twice I had to slow down and dodge around a rabbi, and it actually felt fitting, like we were all intruding on his Sunday morning routine and it's we runners who should be apologising.

Take all the cars out of Brooklyn, like they do on Marathon Sunday, and it looks much the same as it did in the 1970s. You half expect to see a young John Travolta rolling out of a disco, dressed in that pristine white suit from *Saturday Night Fever*.

Then another big bridge, the Pulaski, the second of five, taking us from Brooklyn to Queens and three pleasant miles in a quiet, residential suburb with no barriers separating runners from spectators. The signs being held up here are genuinely funny:

'I've been training for months to hold this sign'.

'You run better than the government'.

'Pain is just the French word for bread'.

'All toenails go to heaven!'

'Worst parade ever!'

We're beyond halfway now and legs are tiring. Mine are long since shot to pieces. I'm struggling. I'd been hoping for a fast time and I'd certainly put in the training, but I knew the game was up as early as the second mile when my legs felt strangely flat while running downhill across the Verrazzano-Narrows Bridge. It usually takes far longer for a marathon to start to sting.

Starting as I did with the fast runners at the front, each mile thereafter becomes an exercise in trying to limit the number of people going past me. Little things are getting to me – the headwind, the undulations. Mostly, I think I'm struggling to find any sort of rhythm after the earlier stress about finding the right bus. Amazing, really, how a moment of anxiety before the start can unravel an entire marathon.

It's why many adopt strategies to calm nerves and focus minds on the start line. Some of my favourites are listed in the Race Day section.

Long Island City in Queens is linked to the Upper East Side of Manhattan by the huge, cantilevered Queensboro Bridge. When the marathon course takes a sharp left and turns up its notorious incline, my race is floundering to such an extent that I'm tempted to slow to a walk.

No question, the climb up the bridge is the most difficult part of the New York City Marathon. However, it's also the coolest. Suddenly, after the noise and general Big Apple-ness of the preceding 15 miles, everything goes quiet. The only sound is your own breathing loud in your ears, along with the pounding, insistent drumbeat of thousands of footsteps echoing off the iron roof of the bridge, 40 metres above the chill waters of the East River.

And then, after the quiet, the wall of noise. You descend onto Manhattan's First Avenue and the soulful stillness is swallowed by the swell of rowdy supporters. The people who choose to cheer here know they're the first human voices runners have heard for over a mile and they take their motivation seriously. You'll struggle to find a louder marathon crowd anywhere in the world. It's quite a tonic – the pep talk we all need. Rocket fuel even for my shredded legs. The thundering shouts of support carry you all the way up First Avenue.

Into the Bronx, where crowds are a little thinner and runners tend to focus inwards. Am I okay for fuel and water? Do I need one of my motivational mantras? There are bands and dancers to help distract us from our fatigue, before we return to Manhattan via the Madison Avenue Bridge – and more comedy handmade signs: *'Last damn Bridge'*.

By now, I'm hanging. But nearly there now, through Harlem, down Fifth Avenue, slowing to a walk every time there's a drink on offer, asking for tea at one point and being looked at like a total fruitcake. Then finally, a right turn into Central Park, where two tricky, rolling, chaotic miles later, the race ends.

I think back to the morning's madness as I'm handed my finisher's medal. True enough, I haven't run as fast as I wanted and much of the marathon felt like a slog. But I nearly never started, almost missed the bus – literally. Many of the others in our party also struggled, while Paula had a whale of a time on the back of a motorbike following the elites, commentating for US television.

Who cares that the race was hard? Better to run, suffer and finish than not even begin. Process over results, as the top athletes will tell you. Journey over destination. And the New York City Marathon is nothing if not a journey.

A magnificent, big, brash, colourful, noisy journey.

THE MAN IN CHARGE

Tip: Do listen to pre-race briefings. They can only help.

I'm proud to be an ambassador for the Manchester Marathon. I run it every year, but **Nick Rusling** *runs* it. Under his guidance, the event has grown from 8,000 runners in 2015 to 25,000 registered in 2020. That makes it the second-biggest marathon in the UK and sixth-biggest in Europe. Known worldwide as the 'fast, flat and friendly' marathon, it's extremely popular with both runners and locals. And as it turns out, running it is a lot easier than *running* it.

I've been organising mass participation events for 19 years, but only really understood the power and emotion attached to a marathon when we bought Manchester.

First, we had to understand the participant. Really getting a feel for a marathon runner. What are they getting out of it? Genuinely, it is different to a half-marathon, to an Olympic-distance triathlon, to a 100-mile bike ride. It's just the power of the brand of marathon, gets into people's souls. And particularly in this country, where you've got the whole charitable angle, more people know that you're doing it. So you're quite exposed as a person. You're putting your soul out there a bit when you're doing a marathon, because everyone goes wow a bit. Particularly obviously if it's your first one. There's just different levels of emotion around marathons. So for me, it's appreciating that because if I don't appreciate that then I can't put on the best event for these people.

Next, you need a route. And that's actually a pretty intelligent bit of work. You have to have a real feel for traffic management. It's not just about going past the best sites, you've got to start with a viewpoint of a pernickety councillor or nimby local. Especially if it's going to be a global marathon, you've got to strike a balance between making the route the absolute best it can be, and minimal disruption.

Sometimes the local disruption is just a natural consequence. But you have to look at, should we do this left rather than that left, we could free up that particular island with residents who would otherwise be blocked, so you've really got to look at it from the lens of traffic flow.

You then have to get all your stakeholders on board, the local councils to start with. And then bus organisers, public transport, police. And the way we approach it, you've got to speak to them individually and sort out their individual issues so when you then stand in a room in front of all these massively influential people in Manchester and ask if there are any issues, you know that there shouldn't be any.

They don't all have to love it, but they have to believe that it's not going to cause chaos. The politicians have to be sure they're not going to lose votes because of their support. Equally, you'll find some passionate people who say fantastic, and can we get schools involved? So you work out what's important to them in a positive sense as well. We have an office in Manchester, the local love is key.

Once you've got the foundations in place, you can look at the two lenses. One is, continue with the operational side, so all the work that goes into staging a safe, successful event. So there's the practical stuff, there's all the different supplies, barriers, loos, medical, traffic-management personnel. We'll have about 1,500 people who work for us. We have about 800 volunteers, which is pretty much a full-time job, just to go to either volunteer groups or sports clubs. We work with loads of the local clubs in Manchester and we give them a bursary, which they can spend on equipment or coaching. All of these different components.

Making sure everyone is briefed on event day with the right inform-ation on where to be, what their role is. If something goes wrong and somebody's brief was incorrect, it massively comes back, everything comes back to me ultimately.

As you get closer and closer to event day, the intensity ramps up. Making sure everyone's been briefed, where to be and when, in that crazy four-hour intense period. There's a certain amount you can do on the Saturday, but fundamentally, there's about a four-hour period, prior to everyone arriving, say seven o'clock first arrivers, because they have a nine o'clock start. You've got teams everywhere, but everything is people knowing exactly where they should be. We have this nerve centre having control, which is fascinating.

We have a nerve centre in Manchester, Trafford Council, just making sure – ticking, ticking, ticking – everything from car park arrivals to trams. And then you build, you build, and the people arrive.

You've also got the marketing. Getting into the spirit of the event; what's the event about? How do we tell people about it? And in current marketing, it's great, because you can just tell different messages to different people. First-timers and/or people who want PBs sub three hours. It used to be one advert in *Men's Health*, you hope that the photo you use is going to serve every purpose. But now you can repurpose things depending on what you want.

And then the other big, big piece is the experience people get. It's not just the roads, the start line and the finishing line. People expect a bit of entertainment. So what's the right extent of what people care about, what are people going to talk about, that helps marketing, 'Ah, this is the event that does something really cool.' And that's the Holy Grail if you've got something that people talk about – it's what I call 'pub chat'.

But we're a marathon. You don't want to take too much from the purity of the marathon message because, as I said at the start, there's something magical about it being a marathon. But, equally, people need help – there are points in the marathon where you need pick-ups.

With a 26-mile route, you can do quite a lot. And, again, it's Manchester. The personality of Manchester. We've got a music area, we've got a football area, we've got an area which is basically there for the communities and councils, we've got a school area and then we've got music and bands and entertainment. And then we've got the last mile, that last finishing moment, and it's a balance between you having your own moment, but also then a celebration.

My own role once the race is underway should be generally bliss-fully calm. If my phone rings, it's bad. I organised the first London triathlon and the cock-up was so big, we made into *A Question of Sport*'s top three funniest clips ever from 50 years of What Happens Next? The elites were basically taken down a dead end. The three women end up coming first, second and third. And our race director, live on *Grandstand*, looking flummoxed down the dead end. We had to pay all the fourth, fifth and sixth the same as if they had come first, second and third – that made page three of *The Times*.

I also created Run to the Beats, which was the first half-marathon in London. First year was a complete mess. It was the first year of social media really becoming a thing and there were a whole load of cock-ups. And so my name's mud, it was like 'Nick Rusling should resign' on social media, and I was a bit hungover after the event and you then think, What do I do? Do I resign? But I think I've got the hang of it now. And I love the finish line. I love the incredible moments that everyone individually is going through and the fact that I've been able to help get them there.

GOODWOOD

Tip: Remember the 10 per cent rule. When ramping up your training, never increase the length or duration of your long run, or your total mileage, by any more than 10 per cent per week.

You never regret a run. It's kind of my mantra that, the words I live by. And I stand by it: assuming no injury, you never do regret a run. But boy did I come close one morning in the beautiful Sussex Downs.

I was running a marathon for the second weekend in a row. I didn't mean to, but somehow my friend and colleague Chris Evans decided he needed another half as a warm-up for New York (Chris is an ace runner and gobbles up at least two marathons a year) and wondered if I fancied coming along to Goodwood.

I have a rule, it slightly annoys me sometimes but I do obey it, that I'll never run a half if there's the option of doing a full marathon. So, having agreed to accompany Chris to Goodwood, instead of running 13.1 miles with him, I found myself signing up for the full 26.2.

The previous week's marathon was off-road and delightful in beautiful, undulating Surrey countryside. If anything, the scenery around Goodwood is even prettier; if you were making a film set in charming Victorian countryside, this is where you'd come.

The marathon and half-marathon are part of a morning's running jamboree around the famous motor circuit which hosts the annual Goodwood Festival of Speed and Goodwood Revival. A clockwise loop of 2.4 miles, with a few mild undulations and seven gentle corners, it's a wonderful venue for two of British summer's most iconic motoring events.

It's also quite fun to run around the first time. And the second. Even the third is okay, but by the fourth, it's not only getting old, you've already begun dreading all the many, many laps still to come. Eleven of them in total.

You must go on. I can't go on. I'll go on.

Mind you for some people, more enlightened souls than me, a lapped course adds another dimension. There are even those who choose to run marathons around a standard athletics track – run 400 metres and repeat 105.5 times. A friend once ran an organised marathon entirely in a disused multi-storey car park in Worthing, 26.2 miles over 71 circuits and 11 levels. And there's those hardy few who find self-transcendence each summer running around the same New York City block 6,000 times.

But it's not for me. Eleven laps of a motor circuit is proving problematic and I'm grinding out the miles. Trouble is, the easier – and slower – you run, the longer it all takes.

This is the second time I've run a marathon of many laps and I didn't much enjoy the first. That day, many years ago on a cycle track in Kent, I was hoping to break three hours for the first time. I'd been putting myself through what can only be described as weekly treadmill torture in training. The Power Hour is the brainchild of an inspirational coach called Rory Coleman, who not only knows his stuff but has been there, done it, got the finisher's tee shirt. He's a veteran of over 1,000 marathons.

Rory's Power Hour consists of 12 five-minute chunks on the treadmill, run back-to-back with no breaks. You run four minutes fast, at goal marathon pace or quicker (around 9 mph in my case), followed by a minute of sprinting (11 mph). Then recover back at marathon pace. And repeat. I once ran it so hard, I started bleeding from the top of my nose.

I was in shape to break three hours on that Saturday morning of my previous multi-lap marathon, but I'd managed to mess it all up during the taper. I'd gone back to the treadmill a couple of days before Race Day and inadvertently overdone it. Basically, I was showing off to myself, delighted with how fast and far I could run, and momentarily forgetting the bigger picture. When it came to the marathon 48 hours later, I blew up something rotten. I was bang on track up until halfway, after which I simply couldn't keep up with the required pace. Every lap was slower than the last and I essentially spent the second half of the marathon sulking. The temptation was immense, every time I passed the place my car was parked, to throw my toys out of the pram and stop. I did finish, but did so with an inward scowl.

Today is different. I'm not cross and I'm not aiming for any particular time. I'm simply, for the first time ever while running, plain bored.

When I was at school, I used to get bored and daydreaming would come to my rescue. I'm sorry, Mr Wicker, but I was rarely present during double maths on a Monday morning, I was Mr Daydream, escaping the jaws of crocodiles and flying on the backs of giant birds while you were explaining the important business of quadratic equations. But bored during a run? This has never happened before. I once ran for 30 hours straight, 153 miles, mostly on uninspiring Greek tarmac, and never once was I bored. For me the whole point of running, or certainly one of the main ones, is that I'm always in the moment – marathons are my mindfulness.

But I'm struggling today. There are miles-to-go markers dotted around the circuit and it's difficult to stay present when every few strides you're bombarded with information which isn't even relevant 90 per cent of the time. During Lap 1, you're looking out for the markers at Miles 1 and 2. But 3 to 26 are also dotted around the course, almost seeming to mock you. Plus, there are markers for the 20-mile race, half-marathon, 10k and 5k. And runners in each of those races too. Constantly you're either overtaking others or being overtaken by runners who may or may not be in the same race. You're losing count of the laps to go. And you're still running clockwise around the same 2.4 miles of asphalt.

Now please don't get me wrong. The race is superbly organised and staffed by the usual brilliant brigade of volunteers. The problem is not with the race itself. The problem lies squarely with me and my seeming inability to cope with multi-lap marathons.

Quite late on, I realise I've been miscounting. Perhaps I should have been concentrating during maths after all, Mr Wicker. Because instead of one lap to go, I discover I have two. The thought briefly crosses my mind to finish a lap early, but of course I'd never forgive myself if I did.

So I steel myself for one final 15–20-minute effort and suddenly grasp what I've been missing. Because there's joy to be had in a race like this, if only you stop resisting it.

The fact you pass the same place over and over again means you get to see friends and family much more often than you do in a normal race. You're never more than 2.4 miles from an aid station, or from the raucous start/finish area. And actually, if I'd only bothered to lift my head and look out, the scenery surrounding the circuit is stunning.

I'm a little cross with myself because I forgot to be grateful. I'm so lucky to be able to enter and enjoy these races, and it seems criminal to run them with no sense of fun, sport or adventure.

By the time I complete the final lap, I'm tempted to do another, just for the hell of it. I stay on the left-hand side of the track, away from the finish funnel, preparing myself for another loop.

But then I remember we're reconvening for a well-deserved, all-afternoon lunch nearby – and the pub wins. I swerve right and accept a medal I feel I barely deserve. Hey ho, lesson learned. And off to the pub.

THE WOMAN WHO RUNS IN BARE FEET

'Run with energy.
Run with lightness.
Run with childlike qualities and your mind won't bother you as much.'
Unknown

You can't miss **Anna McNuff**. She's the one with the bright pink hair running around in bare feet. She describes herself as an adventurer, speaker and mischief maker. She ran the London Marathon barefoot before embarking on a 100-marathon barefoot journey from the very top to the very bottom of Britain. She's an absolute delight, even on email – which she'll sign off with 'a great big running high five at ya!'

The running barefoot seed was in my head because I'd read *Born to Run*, like so many people, and always struggled with shin splints. I just got used to having shin splints all the time, then I realised actually, that's not normal when I shouldn't always be in pain when I was running. So, I guess when I started reading about minimalist running, I was quite open, a bit desperate.

I started out with minimalist shoes and my injuries got less. I felt better when I ran so I thought, this suits me better. I then wore Vivos, very minimal shoes with zero drop from heel to toe, for doing all my running and also walking around in every day.

Then when I went to run the length of New Zealand, I noticed that kids at school were barefoot until they were about 11, especially on the North Island. I just remember looking at their feet and thinking I was jealous because they looked so free. They're kids, so they look free and happy anyway, but it just brought me back to that feeling of being a kid with no shoes on your feet and that sense of running down the sweet shop as fast as you can. I guess that's what I love about adventures, they always get me back to that part of myself, so I looked at being barefoot as trying to get me back to being closer to a kid, basically.

I did six months of just building my mileage up in my Vivos. Then I did six months in these sock things called Skinners, which are halfway between a minimalist shoe and barefoot. Then I just went for it every day, eventually running the length of the UK. Starting in the Shetland Islands and ending five months and 2,352 miles later in London. The first few days were really sore. For the first week, I was sleeping 12 hours a night, and my feet were in bits. Not broken skin, but really, really sore. And, it probably took about three weeks before my feet stopped being incredibly sore every night. With that, they started to toughen up as well – they got a bit more leathery.

You're closer to nature when you're running barefoot. I probably don't tell enough people that. There's no substitute for being able to feel absolutely every contour of the earth when you're running over it – it's very close to ice swimming. People do ice swimming not to see how far they can swim, but for the sensation of it. Similarly, barefoot running suddenly gives you this whole heightened experience.

There's been so much about the benefits of barefoot for injury prevention, but at the end of the day, it's that feeling. It's very pure. It's very human. In our world where we're told what to buy and this technical thing and that technical thing, the idea of just me and nature ... It's beautiful and simple, isn't it?

I was in the Yorkshire Dales and running up a mountain. It was just before the end of the day and I was going to run over the top of the mountain and down into the valley and spend the night at a pub. I was just tanking it up. It was really hard work, but I got to the top just as the sun was going down. It was really peaceful and quiet. I could see the Dales, the sheep in the fields, it was golden hour. And the surface was beautiful. I felt so alive. I just thought, this is amazing, what a pleasure.

It's pretty special, although sometimes that means you're touching stuff you don't much want to. Although, do you know what? Poo did not bother me in the slightest. Dog poo is the worst, because it's really sticky and it stinks whereas sheep poo, cow poo, horse poo, I was not bothered by any of that. Sheep poo does this thing: it sort of does a nuclear mushroom between your toes when you stand on it. It's very explosive. I wasn't bothered by any of that. The worst stuff was glass. It's all the stuff that's manmade, I didn't mind the stuff nature had made.

Except, one day I did get lost. I had my phone out to see where I was going and I stepped backwards along this quiet back road and I stood in something really cold and wet. I thought it was just poo or grass or mud, but I looked down and I'd walked into the stomach of a dead rabbit – I just hit the roof!

Running a big city marathon barefoot like London was awesome! I was pretty stoked with 3hrs 44 in bare feet. I'm not entirely sure how that happened. Probably because: I LOVED IT. And high fives all round for Girlguiding.

Being barefoot, it just elevates it. I try and describe it to people like, imagine you've spent your whole life wearing gloves and gone on your hands and gone through your whole life wearing gloves in your daily life. Then, you take those gloves off. Suddenly, you just feel everything so much more. I really get off on those physical sensations. It's like a rush. It's addictive, that feeling of being able to feel everything you're running over and pushing off your foot and knowing there is nothing between you and the ground. It just feels awesome.

The growing popularity of Vaporflys is odd. We love new shiny things, don't we? And I sympathise with that. If someone is a hobby runner, with only a limited time to run and to train, transitioning to being a barefoot runner takes an awful lot of time. You probably also have to allow your split times and speed to go backwards before they pick back up again. I think people just don't want to give it that time. They're impatient. They've got an hour a day, three times a week, to go out and do their runs and they want a quick fix. We all want that silver bullet. That's why self-help books are so popular, isn't it? What's the one thing that I can do now that's going to fix my life tomorrow? And it doesn't exist.

People mistakenly feel like they need more and more support to give them less and less pain. Actually, at the end of the day, maybe trust your body a bit more. You know your body better than anyone else, just test a few things out and listen to what your body's telling you.

AMSTERDAM

Tip: If you're stuck in a running rut, think about whether you're working too hard on easy days, or too easy on hard days.

Like many others alongside me on the start line in Amsterdam, I've come here for a PB. And a thumping big one at that.

This is the culmination of a 10-month quest. It's my second bite at this particular cherry after a slower-than-planned spring marathon. I'm determined to put that right in the autumnal Dutch capital. I've ticked all the boxes, even boxes that don't really need ticking.

They say people who start running in middle age – like me – only keep improving for the first seven years. After that, it's a gradual, steady descent. In Amsterdam I'm well over a decade into my running journey, grateful for every second of it, but determined to persuade my legs to propel me to one final hurrah.

I once ran a small-time marathon near Milton Keynes in 2:55, the quickest I've ever managed. Actually, 2:55:56, but the seconds are always free. However, I always suspected the course was a bit short. Certainly my Garmin insisted it was, as did several fellow runners. So, when I broke three hours (by less than a minute) in London the following year, I decided that would be my 'official' PB. I know for a fact that London, as one of the six World Marathon Majors, would not come up short. Also, somewhat easier to shoot at 2:59 than 2:55.

Since then I graduated to longer races, 50 miles, 100 miles, multi-day mountain ultras, so I developed another weapon in my running armoury – a new understanding of pain. I could train harder than ever before.

Ten months ago I set about speed training with gusto. I'd finish work on the breakfast show and run my commute home – just over 10 pleasant, riverside miles along the Thames towpath. I hit them hard.

I frequently ran myself so ragged that I collapsed, exhausted, onto the pavement outside our house – unable to stay upright, gasping for breath, exhilarated by how far I pushed my limits. First time it happened, my wife Caroline mopped me up and hurried me inside before the neighbours could notice. But soon the sight of me quietly drowning in a pool of lactate and sweat became commonplace. I trained like a man possessed. Tempo runs, interval runs, hard fartlek sessions … I broke my new work-to-home record. Then broke it again. And again. They say train hard, fight easy. Well, I've never trained harder. I entered a flat spring marathon and impatiently counted the hours until the start. It was going to be a victory lap.

Except, it wasn't.

It began okay, but after 14 miles, my legs simply couldn't keep up with the required pace and I struggled home 10 minutes slower than planned. It took me all of an hour to get over it. On the train home, still wearing my medal somewhat desultorily round my neck, I resolved to redouble my training and aim for a fast autumn marathon. As one of my favourite running songs says, *I get knocked down, but I get up again.*

To Amsterdam then, the flattest marathon in Europe, and surely a new *'persoonlijk record'*. More tempo runs. More lactate. More interval sessions. More pavement collapses. A summer vacation featuring hills, more hills, and mountains. All run up hard. All for a few seconds off my marathon time.

Autumn arrived, the final month and a half before Amsterdam, and my long training runs became actual marathons. Five of them, three hilly and two flat, all run just hard enough – but taking care not to take too much out of the legs.

During race week, I sometimes struggle to keep the miles down, but for Amsterdam I observed the taper impeccably. I cut alcohol completely. And even though I knew full well that the old-fashioned carb-starve/carb-load model has been scientifically discredited, I did it anyway. I ate only protein and fats on Monday and Tuesday, before gradually increasing the proportion of carbohydrates to a climax on Friday and Saturday. I packed caffeinated energy gels, which disagree with me *bigly*, just in case.

Then on the eve of the marathon, on a whim, I spent a fortune on a pair of new trainers.

It's the Kenyans' fault, that last one. Them and Nike.

You see the previous weekend Eliud Kipchoge became the first person in history to run a marathon in under two hours. I watched on my phone, holding our five-year-old daughter Mary's hand as she attempted her first senior parkrun, while Kipchoge wowed the world, crossing the finish line in Vienna in 1:59:40. And I wept. It was wonderful. The marathon that was also a sprint.

The following day, another Kenyan, Brigid Kosgei, broke Paula Radcliffe's 16-year-old women's world record. Shattered it. Paula's record set in London in 2003 stood at 2:15:25. In over 16 years, nobody had come close. Not even within a minute and a half. Then Kosgei rocks up in Chicago and calmly runs 2:14:04, lowering the record by fully 81 seconds. Probably inspired by – and in its way every bit as impressive as – the achievement in Vienna the previous morning.

And what did Kosgei and Kipchoge have in common – apart from their country of birth and prodigious talent? Nike's controversial new shoe, whose soles have carbon-fibre plates designed to help runners spring forward off the road with each stride. Independent research found these shoes improved efficiency by 4 per cent compared with regular trainers, hence the name Vaporfly 4%. One of the top amateur American runners in Chicago, unsponsored, bought the shoes and surprised everybody, most of all himself, by finishing in the top 10. He said it felt like running on a trampoline.

Others aren't so sure. Ryan Hall, the first American to run a marathon in under 2:05, refuses to believe that the Vaporfly even counts as a shoe: 'It's a spring, and a clear mechanical advantage.' Sara Hall, Ryan's wife and an elite distance runner herself, says, 'Honestly, it's a bummer. It's hard to just celebrate performances at face value.' Former New York Road Runners president Mary Wittenberg goes further. 'I actually think we're going to have asterisks on all the results that are like AV and BV – Before Vaporfly.' And my favourite quote comes from Desiree Linden, the Brooks-sponsored winner of the 2018 Boston marathon: 'It's an arms race,' she proclaimed.

'When it should be a foot race.' Several months later, World Athletics are criticised for ruling the Vaporfly race legal.

In a shady corner of the Amsterdam expo, somebody is selling speed. I dither, but only for a moment. Soon, I'm giddily handing over an obscene amount of money for a pair of those time-shifting pink trainers. They cost roughly double the next most expensive running shoe, but it's a small price to pay for a 4 per cent boost in performance. Because even I can work out that 4 per cent faster than 2:59 is 2:51 and beyond my wildest dreams.

Amsterdam Sunday morning dawns and I'm ready. Determined. Confident. Also, humble. In my hotel room before breakfast, I practise yoga to keep my feet on the ground – ironically, by flinging them in the air and doing a headstand. I stretch, breathe, meditate, resolve to stay in the moment. Then I remember Dr Costas, the sport psychology professor who tells us in the Music section that songs can be like legal doping, and I grab my trusty iPod before I leave the room. Add some banging tunes into the mix and I might even sneak under 2:50.

As I lace up my lurid new trainers and walk purposefully to the start, I'm secretly convinced I'm going to smash this. Well, to paraphrase the climber, there are only two types of marathon. Hard, and bloody hard. Amsterdam proves bloody hard.

After the very first mile I know it won't be my day. The music, shoes and gels. The yoga, the taper. The carb-starving. The 10 long months of lung-busting training. My confidence. All evaporate into nothing when I run the first mile 30 seconds slower than I need to.

I reach for an energy gel in the hope I can defibrillate myself. You make kind of a deal with the devil when you squeeze energy gels into your mouth mid-race, especially caffeinated ones. They do offer the seductive promise of a quick mile or two, but boy, do you pay the price later. When you cross the finish line, and for the rest of the day, it feels like World War III is being waged inside your stomach. And all those shots of caffeine? Well, you can forget sleep tonight.

But in those pancake-flat streets of Amsterdam, perfect for fast times, I'm at DEFCON 1. I down gel after gel after gel. Usually, I carry one or two sachets for emergency use only. Today, leaving nothing to chance, I've brought five – and down the lot greedily. I spend the first six miles in a fog of sugar, caffeine and self-delusion. But the prospect of a PB, along with my belief in my own running, is ebbing away.

The Amsterdam Marathon begins and ends in the grand old Olympic stadium used for the Games of 1926. Locals say the cauldron which housed the Olympic flame looks like a giant ashtray, but I think it looks stately. The course meanders alongside canals and through the city centre, bisects the mile-long Vondelpark and thrillingly invites you to run right through the middle of the Rijksmuseum. The bulk of the route is by the banks of the River Amstel. By the time my brain has caught up with my legs and I can bear to admit to myself that all PB hope is lost, I'm running between windmills, grand riverside houses and DJs on barges, trying to encourage runners with deafening Dutch house music.

I appreciate the gesture, but the music has the opposite effect on me. Fellow runners stream past and I try desperately to hang onto their coat tails. But always fail.

I cast around for someone to blame. Or something to pin this crushing disappointment on. I feel like blaming everybody who overtakes me. Or this thundering music, which ordinarily would make me smile.

Or how about these lurid shoes? Yes, especially these preposterous pink shoes. They're everywhere, like some kind of contagion.

So many runners with the same idea as I had, to buy a 4 per cent improvement in finishing time. In my heartbroken head, this now seems like an immoral extravagance. Paying for speed feels like cheating. If this is the way our sport is going, I tell myself, away from its simple soul, then I decide I want nothing to do with it.

Mind you, it seems I'm alone in these thoughts. The pink shoes just keep coming. Among the faster club runners looking for a sub-3 finish time, almost a quarter look to have paid out the big bucks. Even as I drop back through the field, Vaporflys keep springing past me. It's only a week since Kipchoge and Kosgei, Nike must be beside themselves with glee.

Not me though. I'm rank miserable. I've got almost 20 miles still to run and I know they'll all be what I call treacle miles – like you're wading through knee-high treacle. And so they prove. However, the agonies in my legs pale into insignificance compared to the turbulence going on in my head. I can't help but focus on how far there is to go; 19 miles seems like forever. It's definitely too far. The thought even occurs to me to simply stop running. I never think like this! It must be the pressure I've been piling on myself.

Of course I do know that I can – and doubtless will – reach the finish line. My single DNF (Did Not Finish) came in a

Welsh mountain wilderness after three days and many excruciating miles on an increasingly injured ankle. And I didn't give up that day, I was pulled from the race with an ankle the size of a basketball, my whole leg looking like it had been turned upside down. Comparatively, a couple more hours on horizontal city streets adorned with music, cheering crowds and frequent aid stations should be a walk in the park.

Which is exactly what's making this so difficult. That, and the unwelcome thought that my fastest days are almost certainly now behind me. I suppose it was always going to hit home like this, in the middle of a running race, the blunt bodily business of growing older, weaker, slower … Mae West famously quipped, 'They don't make mirrors like they used to.' Well, they don't make Garmins like they used to either.

My mind is churning. I set myself ever more disheartening targets. Reluctantly I despair of going sub-3. Soon, it becomes clear that 3:05 is beyond me and so I focus – for what little it's worth – on breaking 3:10. This is so much slower than my projected time, over 30 seconds-a-mile slower, that I relax a little and try to make tentative friends with the fact that I can still run a marathon in three oh-something.

I cross the line in 3:12. Exhausted. Embarrassed.

I do obviously know that my marathon PB is a matter of importance only to me. Nobody's going to like me more if I can run a marathon faster than 2:59. In fact they'll probably *dislike* me for moaning about 3:12. Even so, I feel a pressing need to exorcise the crushing frustration of the last 192 minutes, the past 10 months of bespoke training, and Amsterdam provides the perfect opportunity.

The full marathon begins at 9 a.m., while the much-bigger half starts, bizarrely, at 1 p.m. on a wide, tree-lined avenue just outside the Olympic Stadium. After picking up my medal and swapping the expensive new trainers for some trusty old ones, I sneak into the starting pen for the half. Nobody questions me, I'm wearing a race number after all.

It's naughty, a spur-of-the-moment decision. I have a vague notion of jogging round with some of our travelling party who'd signed up for 13.1 miles instead of the full 26.2, but I can't find any of them in the melee. It's no bad thing, I need time to myself. Time to think. Time to come to terms with my time.

As I run through Amsterdam for the second time in as many hours, I gain some much-needed perspective. We all age, we all weaken. The trick of course is to suck the life out of every moment, to appreciate it. Here are two of the key lessons running has taught me:

Life is about the journey.
The joy is in the struggle.

And on the streets of eastern Amsterdam, running was gently reminding me of those.

When I finish back in the stadium, I refuse a second medal, and later, after a shower, bounce into our post-race party. I'm still disappointed not to have broken my PB (of course I am), but far from mourning my performance or raging against the fading of the light, I feel strangely reborn.

The miles may be going into slow motion, but I'm grateful they're still going.

THE MAN WHOSE MARATHON WAS CANCELLED BUT HE RAN IT ANYWAY, AROUND HIS GARDEN, DRESSED AS A RHINOCEROS

'Divide the marathon into thirds. Run the first part with
your head, the middle part with your personality,
and the last part with your heart.'
Mike Fanelli, champion marathon runner and coach

One of the best things about running marathons is the friends you make along the way. In 2017, seven strangers all bid for VIP places at two major marathons, raising money for Children in Need. They all ran London, then they all ran New York. They stayed in touch and have now become life-long pals. You've never seen a busier WhatsApp group. **Andy Humphries** was one of them. He's a talented runner with a sub-3 hour marathon PB, who's also completed the gruelling

135-mile Badwater Ultramarathon. Above all, he's a lovely human being.

Andy was training to run London 2020 in a massive rhino suit when all marathons were postponed or cancelled because of the coronavirus pandemic. He decided to run 26.2 miles on the day anyway, 200 laps of his garden dressed as a rhinoceros.

Once you've done a few marathons and longer-distance races, you look for the next challenge. The rhino costumes have become iconic and they always feature on the television coverage. Also, it's a conservation charity I'm interested in and I wanted to do something inspirational for my son Jack, something I could go out to schools and talk about.

It's not light. It's about 10 kilos, but that's not the issue really. The rhino costumes were originally donated to the charity from a West End show about 20 years ago, so they're certainly not designed for running. You put this big metal frame on and it's cumbersome, quite uncomfortable. And then you Velcro it up and strap yourself in, and there's these little ledges that hold the head. Now, the head is quite heavy so it pulls you forward. When you're running, if you don't hold the head, it bangs around all the time.

So, first thing is, you're running with your hands in front of you and you have to do that the whole way. All the time the head is pulling you forward as you hold on to keep it still. The other thing is, outside the metal frame, it's rubbery – like bits of wetsuit. So it does get pretty hot in there. And because you've got discrepancy between the top of the head and the bottom of the costume, your visibility is restricted. When you first get in the thing, you wonder how you're ever going to run in it. You do get used to it a little bit, but it takes a bit more out of your upper body than you think, because you're carrying the weight and holding the head.

The charity said, 'Don't run in it too much beforehand, because you'll be put off. The crowd will get you through.'

I did two parkruns in it, Burnham and Long Ashton in Bristol. You sense straight away that you're going to get a lot of support. You see people coming towards you, even the guy that's leading, applauding you and saying, 'Come on, rhino.' Also, lots of selfies. You are the celebrity of that race, which helps massively – and you imagine how much extra support there'll be for you in a race like London. But after 5k, you're getting very, very sweaty and things are aching that don't normally ache when you run. A marathon is eight and a half 5k parkruns.

Then London inevitably had to be postponed due to the coronavirus pandemic and you think, c'est la vie, really. Hey-ho, I will keep training. I was disappointed of course, massively disappointed, but there were bigger issues here. Nothing I can do about it and they postponed for all the right reasons. At that point, I hadn't considered doing it around the garden, that came a little bit later.

Captain Tom was my inspiration. I watched him walk 100 laps of his garden aged 99, and just thought, I have done all this training. I am ready to do this. Let's try the marathon around the garden.

Running around the garden is a lot, lot slower, with all the twists and turns, running on the grass and up and down a hill. It was seven and a half laps per mile. It starts by the house, a little bit of patio, up onto the grass, round the lawn, down onto a gravel drive, around past the house on a gravel path, and then back to the start. Almost 200 laps. You just get into a rhythm and there's other things going on in your mind. How long is this taking me? When am I going to have a drink? When am I going to eat a gel? When am I going to stop for a pee break?

I knew there would be a couple of people around, but there was loads of support. And of course, this wasn't general support for people in the London Marathon. This was support for me, just me.

People used their permitted daily exercise to come to our gate at the one end and our neighbours were looking over the fence at the other.

I was due to start at half past six in the morning, and at quarter past, the friends I made running the London and New York marathons three years previously all dialled in for a Zoom call to motivate me. And while I was running, they went and did a virtual marathon between them.

Actually, I had people call me on Zoom throughout and I would run along and I'd say hi on the computer screen as I passed. So, there was a lot of people involved really, in person and online, cheering me on. Lots of support to take my mind off the monotony.

There was a guy next door who'd been seriously ill. He managed to get out to applaud me and said he felt much better afterwards.

At one point I climbed the hill for one lap of the village. People were all out banging saucepans and had banners saying 'Well Done, Andy'. We collected money en route. And it was just like my own special marathon to the point where I think it was better than actually doing London. So those things made it a day. It was fantastic. Someone asked me afterwards, 'Was it the toughest marathon?' No, not really, a lot because of all of that support.

As I finished, the 2017 London and New York marathon lot were back on Zoom, cheering me on, along with a few people leaning over the fence. It took me six and a half hours. When I finished, it was sheer relief. And pride. I honestly enjoyed every second.

Would I recommend it? Absolutely. Would I recommend that you did it in a costume? Well, once you've done a marathon or two or three, you will look for another challenge and it's a great way to get a charity noticed. It's different. And you get bucketloads of support, which carries you through like nothing else. It's brilliant!

HAMPSHIRE HOPPIT

Tip: Hill running is speed training in disguise.

The hills of Hampshire are in full summer glow. The trees are richly green, preening. In the sky there's drama: it seems to be simultaneously raining and bright. The sun is performing a balancing act, surfing along the edge of a dark cloud, trying not to fall into it. The light is dazzling, but fragile. It's a privilege to be alive on a morning like this.

Except I'm in no state to appreciate any of that. Far less run a marathon. Hungover doesn't begin to do it justice. In fact, terrible as I feel staggering towards the start, I'm not even sure my hangover has properly kicked in yet. The following 26.2 hilly miles, I have no doubt, are going to bite.

Precisely what I was thinking when – sober – I agreed to run a trail marathon on the way home from the year's biggest party, I have no idea. It really *is* on the way home, though, almost exactly equidistant from the New Forest, where I partied last night like it was 1999, and Barnes, where I live. No more than a 15-minute detour off the M3. Perhaps that was the clincher; it was simply too convenient *not to run*. Especially as a friend was doing all the driving.

The friend in question, Chris Peskett, had run another marathon the previous day and wanted to do this too as part of the training for his first 100-miler. He says his legs are shot to pieces, and we spend a happy few minutes on the start line discussing who's in the worse state. I'm confident it's me: to add to the hangover, I've only slept for a matter of minutes.

We agree to run together and help each other through, but never quite manage it. Somehow we lose sight of each other in the congested starting area. One moment Chris is standing right next to me, and the next I'll see of him will be back here at lunchtime as I watch him finish.

The gun goes (a loud bang being the last thing I need in my current state) and we set off straight up a steep hill. The idea for this race was born in a pub – of course it was! – in the nearby village of Little London. I'm told initially the race was going to be called the 'Little London Marathon' – exactly mimicking the Virgin Money London Marathon logo and simply adding the word 'Little'. For legal and logistical reasons, mainly legal, this never happened. And so the Hampshire Hoppit came into being. Hoppit was the beer they were drinking in the pub at the time, and a pint is given to every finisher.

The way I'm feeling puffing up this hill, a pint of beer will pretty much finish me off. I don't often drink heavily and when I do, I don't half suffer for it the next day.

Thank goodness the course is so pretty. I'd never previously heard of the North Wessex Downs but they're glorious. We run through rolling chalk hills, woodland, pasture, heath and common land. There's something about running off-road that sings to the soul.

I wish it would sing to the hangover too. Five miles in, and I'm wondering when (not if) I'm going to throw up. And when (not if) I do, whether it would be okay to do so by the side of the race route. The idea of adding even 20 yards to my morning run is too awful to contemplate. And still more than 20 miles left to go …

I know I won't quit – the determination born in Barcelona at Mile 18 of my first marathon still burns bright. But I do have plenty of time to consider why on earth I'm putting myself through this.

One of my heroes is Emil Zátopek. He was my 'chosen specialist subject' when I went on the BBC TV quiz show *Mastermind*. In running circles, he's referred to in awed terms.

Zátopek was a pioneering runner – perhaps the greatest ever – and an equally fine human being. A Czech soldier by trade, he discovered a groundbreaking way of interval training – essentially, the more the better. He would run 10 miles through deep snow in his army boots, occasionally carrying his wife Dana on his back, and proceed to run as many as 80 (80!) laps of the track flat out, with minimal recovery. And then 10 miles back home through the snow. And this was an era when the British elite considered training to be counter-productive and somewhat vulgar.

Zátopek won gold medals and broke world records for fun. At the 1952 Olympics in Helsinki, he stormed to victory in the 10,000 metres, then won one of the greatest 5,000-metre races in history. Twice he was overtaken on the final lap, and twice he found extra speed from somewhere deep within.

A few days later, on a whim, the 'Czech Locomotive' (as he was known) decided to enter the marathon – even though he'd never previously run the distance. Known for chatting amiably mid-race, Zátopek struck up a conversation with the British world record holder Jim Peters. A conversation that would go down in legend.

'Jim, I've never run this distance before. Are we not going a little too fast?'

They were indeed running fast, 10 miles in, and Peters was feeling it. He snapped back grumpily: 'No, if anything, this pace is too slow.'

At which point Zátopek thanked Peters, duly sped up and shattered the Olympic record by six minutes. He remains the only person to win the long distance treble at the same Games.

Dana won the javelin title in Helsinki. Coincidentally, the couple were born on the same day, married on the same day (obviously) and they also won Olympic gold on the same day. Quite the sporting power couple.

In later life, at great personal cost, Zátopek was a leading figure in the Prague Spring and protester against Soviet occupation. He also once hosted the great Australian distance runner Ron Clarke and gave him a small package wrapped in brown paper as he left. Clarke had broken many of Zátopek's world records, but bad luck and circumstance meant he had never won an Olympic medal.

Clarke opened the package as the plane took off from Prague. It was one of Zátopek's Olympic gold medals with a simple note: 'Because you deserve it'.

That's what I'm thinking about as I trundle along in Hampshire. I'm trying to channel my inner Zátopek: get it done and be charming along the way.

And actually, I do perk up considerably. At about Mile 8, my hangover begins to evaporate and my legs enliven. To be perfectly honest, this happens soon after I drink some flat Coke at an aid station. It's probably the caffeine and sugar that fuel the revival, but I hope it's also inspiration from across the decades. From that moment on, I feel invincible.

One final thing about Zátopek: the way he looked when he was running. Think of Eliud Kipchoge, Zen master – never a flicker of emotion but for the occasional smile when things get tough. Now, reverse it: Zátopek was the exact opposite. Tongue lolling, eyes rolling, face contorted against the agonies shredding every fibre of his being. As the American sportswriter Red Smith noted at the time: *'Zátopek runs like a man with a noose around his neck, the most frightful horror show since Frankenstein.'*

That's me, usually. My running face goes through unspeakable contortions. Strangely, not today. You'd imagine running with a hangover that I'd make Frankenstein look sexy. But for some reason, I'm more Eliud than Emil since I started feeling better. Smiling, not scowling.

I wonder if the dreaded 'Wall' will hit today, and how a hangover will affect that. I recall a conversation with a pal, Rob Owen, head of the St Giles Trust charity. Rob was so terrified of hitting the Wall in his first marathon, that he brought a wall with him. Literally, built a wall on a sledge and dragged it round 26.2 miles of the London marathon.

When you start running all you can hear is this 'cra, cra, cra...' as the sled is pulled over the road. And you quickly become world expert on friction. Bus lanes, not good, extra drag, sticky when it rains. The pavements were okay. Road not as good as the pavements. Cobbles better as the sledge would glide over wet cobbles like it was dancing.

After about four miles there's a gentle uphill. Fellow runners would come along, trying to be kind, and give me a hand. Because obviously it's tough dragging a sledge up a hill. They give the sledge a push, but you don't know they're coming because they're behind you. And suddenly you get this whoosh and you're falling forward. I must've fallen over five times with someone just trying to help. And of course that caused great amusement all around.

I ran every yard. But the crowd gave me so much attention that I didn't run a step on my own. I found that incredibly uplifting. There was always some banter or someone shouting something silly or encouragement - or just surprise.

I did put in a pretty good sprint at the end. But not as fast as the people around me. Nobody wanted to be beaten by the guy dragging a wall!

In Hampshire, there's a long steady hill at Mile 15, goes on for ages. I have a genuine spring in my step as I canter up. My mind feels so clear and my legs so sweet that I imagine I'm leaving a trail behind me as I run.

Why did I sign up for a marathon the morning after the biggest party of the year?

Why wouldn't I?

As I career down the long, straight hill to the finish, I'm wishing the race was longer. I genuinely don't want it to end.

Suddenly, out of nowhere, someone overtakes me. We're vying for something like 11th place, it really doesn't matter who finishes ahead. Yet a competitive streak stirs within me. I'm not having that. He's clearly been shadowing me all the way down the hill, waiting for his moment. Well, pal – you went early. I am Zátopek! I summon every sinew, surge back past him and cross the finish line just in front.

I'm on a high for the rest of the day. Apart from anything else, I'm simply thankful to be caught in the eye of this meteoric rise in running's popularity.

Keen to explore this further, the following morning I call the great commentator and athletics historian Roger Robinson at his home in New Zealand. An excellent athlete in his own right, he then spent many decades travelling the world, watching top-level athletics.

Name any seismic running event in the past 70-odd years, and Roger will have witnessed it in person. He's written a sterling book called *When Running Made History* – because when it did, like I say, he was there.

When Zátopek won his first Olympic gold medal in London in 1948. When Roger Bannister broke the 4-Minute Mile in Oxford in 1956. When Abebe Bikila won the Rome Olympic Marathon barefoot. When Kathrine Switzer (now his wife) became the first woman to run the Boston Marathon in 1967. When Ben Johnson won the men's 100m in Seoul, then tested positive for drugs. When Paula Radcliffe broke the marathon world record in London ... Roger was there.

He can't quite get his head around how popular running has become:

How did this happen? What happened to my little sport, where there used to be about 15 of us and we would leave our tracksuits under the park bench and the first man in stopped the watch?

It's an amazing transformation. It goes right through society. It's an enormous benefit to us, which is why I wanted to write a book about it, dealing with all of that absolutely front-on.

As I sit listening to him, my phone bleeps to tell me about an email from Amazon: *Your item is on its way.* The sort of 'item' which until very recently I'd nip out to the shops for. But, like many others, I've been seduced by the sheer ease of pressing a button and marvelling as whatever I want arrives box-fresh within hours. I wonder if Roger thinks we've all started running as an antidote to the modern world and the mobile phone?

Absolutely. An antidote to the modern world and to the anonymity of it. Huge numbers and people living lives that don't feel very significant, and running does help you feel significant. And in some ways, without overstating this, it has some aspects of a religion, in that it's something which is very individually fulfilling, and a lot of people will say it's spiritually fulfilling. But at the same time, it also has a very strong communal basis and so you do it with groups of other people.

It satisfies those two sides of our nature, while at the same time in a world where the great danger is being sedentary, and just sitting in cars, and sitting in front of computers all the time, running is very simple, and very active, and gets you out there. Also, you're interacting with nature and with the weather. And whatever the conditions, you're out there doing it, and whatever the surface is, you're up there doing it. So, it has all those aspects of being natural and health-giving.

I steer the conversation to Zátopek, that agonised face of his as he ran. Roger watched it live in the 1940s. I wonder aloud whether in this modern, over-comforted, over-convenienced world, perhaps a bit of good old-fashioned pain and effort does us some good?

> I totally agree. I'm 80 now, and when I run races, which I still run as I always have done, as hard as I can, and therefore gasping a bit at the end, and doing a bit of a Zátopek imitation, the young guys, especially in America where they're very compassionate, they say, 'Are you all right, sir? You'll make it.' They think I'm going to die.
>
> In fact, all I'm doing is what I've been doing exactly the same for the last 65 years.

When I'm 80, I hope like Roger I can look back and measure out my life in finisher's medals.

I put a reminder note in the diary:

June 2055. Enter the Hampshire Hoppit marathon.

THE WOMAN WHO SURVIVED THE BOSTON BOMBS, THEN RETURNED TO GET MARRIED MID-MARATHON

'Strength does not come from physical capacity.
It comes from indomitable will.'
Mahatma Gandhi

Susie Comstock celebrated turning 40 by running her first marathon. She celebrated turning 50 by running her 50th. She's completed races all over the USA but her story is defined by Boston: Susie was on the finish line with her partner Dave when the bombs went off. They returned to the city to get married, mid-marathon. And in between, Susie survived cancer.

Boston 2013 was actually going to be a monumental marathon for me because it was going to be my 10th consecutive Boston. When you run 10 straight Bostons, you officially become a 'streaker' with entry privileges for future years. Very monumental for me.

Dave was ahead of me and at Mile 24, I told my two girlfriends to run ahead and please tell him I'll be there shortly. And so I was coming down Boylston Street – and as I always do, I fixed my hair, was primping myself for that finisher picture.

It was literally 2:50 in the afternoon and I was getting ready to cross that finish line when the first bomb went off. And I honestly don't remember what happened except I felt things brushing up against my arm. Crowds on the right-hand side were screaming and scrambling to get out of the stands. Then on the left, I kept hearing just massive screams and I know I stood there for probably, I don't even know, a couple of seconds. There was another woman next to me and I just remember her, instead of to the right of me, all of a sudden in front of me crying, and I'm looking at her face and not understanding what was going on.

And then all of a sudden, they're screaming at us to move forward. My mind shifted too – I need to meet Dave at a certain pole because we had decided where we were going to meet after the marathon since he was finishing before me. I needed to get to that pole. So, I just started running to the pole and as I was running to the pole, I crossed the finish line. I started hearing from behind me on the line, Dave screaming my name and I just looked at him and we just started embracing. And I guess we just continued going through the process of moving forward. There were police coming with their guns, up in the air, just screaming at us to move forward. And then of course we started hearing the sirens and then they pushed us forward to get out of the way of the sirens.

Dave just kept holding me and just saying stay in the middle. I didn't know what happened. He figured out what probably was going on. Move forward, move forward. Get our bags, finally. We stayed at a hotel that was right next door. I was in shock. My son was supposed to be at the far end of the finish line by the hotel. I got up into the room and my phone is going off the wall. People calling, people texting, still in shock, don't know what's happening. Of course, once my son knocks on the hotel-room door and I open it and that's when it hit me.

I couldn't sleep for two days. Then we flew home and I still couldn't sleep that entire week.

Five months later, I was diagnosed with breast cancer. Just going through the emotional ups and downs with Boston, and then five months later, now it's okay, yeah, oh, and by the way, you've got breast cancer. So, we were like, okay, we can handle this.

After I rang the bell for the end of my treatment, we decided to return to the marathon course to get married at Mile 20. We didn't say anything to the Boston Athletic Association because we didn't know if it was legal or not, so we kept that hush-hush.

The meaning behind Mile 20: I have cousins that live in Newton and every year during the marathon, they are always out cheering me on at Mile 20. My very first Boston, my parents came as well. So, Mile 20 was just something that seemed special: to be married where my family is during every marathon that I've run.

Lots and lots of planning. I had ordered some blue and yellow umbrellas. My father paints, so he painted the inside of the umbrellas with flowers. So, it was really magical. We had cousins, we had my parents, we had all of our children. They were all holding the umbrellas and before we arrived, they had to persuade the police officers that had barricaded off the street to open it up. They opened up just one barricade so that we could run in and get married.

I had tee shirts made for us, running shirts, and since Dave and I were going to be side by side. The front of one shirt said Getting Married and then the date and the other shirt said Mile 20 and the date. Then on the back, it was the opposite. So that if you're behind us, or a spectator, you could read Getting Married, Mile 20. Well, once we got married, I had shirts that we put on over since it was so cold. This time they said Just Married and Mile 20.

So, it was fun. It was real fun. So, I carried the flowers, now our running shirts said Just Married, and of course Dave was running on the side of the road, high fiving everybody because they could see I was carrying flowers and they could read our shirts. They were all like, no way, no way! And we were saying thank you all for coming to our wedding! We're so glad you got the invitation! It was just so awesome. The response from people as we were running was fabulous.

Towards the end, I was getting a little nervous because we didn't clear it with the BAA. But we stopped just before the finish line and did a kiss before we crossed the line, a hug and a kiss, and they captured that for us and that was the best finisher picture ever.

So, it was fun. It was a lot of planning and a whole lot of fun.

LONDON

Tip: Don't throw away all your old tops! They add a layer of warmth as you wait in the start line and can be tossed in the charity bins as you start running.

'Twenty-nine thousand people and a million butterflies ...' It's one of the great lines of sports commentary. Vin Scully called Major League Baseball matches for 67 years until he retired in 2016. Those were his evocative, unscripted words as LA Dodgers pitcher Sandy Koufax stepped up to the plate in 1965 and made history with the perfect game:

> *Twenty-nine thousand people and a million butterflies. I would think that the mound at Dodger Stadium right now is the loneliest place in the world. You can almost taste the pressure. Koufax lifts his cap, runs his fingers through his black hair, pulls the cap back down, fussing at the bill. He heaves a sigh, takes a hitch at his belt. He is one out away from the Promised Land.*

But change a word here and there, and this commentary works just as well for the start line of the 2016 London Marathon. My own perfect game:

> *Thirty-nine thousand people and a million butterflies. I would think the start line in Greenwich Park right now is the loneliest place in the world. You can almost taste the pressure. Alexander lifts his cap, runs his fingers through his brown hair, pulls the cap back down, fussing at the bill. He heaves a sigh, takes a hitch at his shorts. He is 26.2 miles away from the Promised Land.*

Usually I adore the atmosphere at the start of any marathon, London in particular. This is my home city and it's never better than on marathon Sunday morning. But today is different. Today, as I say, the butterflies are swarming.

Nobody talks to each other on the tube in London – except on marathon Sunday morning. Everyone's wearing a race number – thus travelling for free – and everyone's excited and nervous. The perfect, heady mix.

'How's your training gone?'

'Is this your first marathon?'

'What time are you hoping for?'

Dare I say it, this is the Underground as it ought to be.

On the way this morning, I spy a packet of Rothmans poking out of a fellow runner's race bag and ask her about it.

> I run this race every year for my local hospice. It takes me almost seven hours. I smoke one cigarette on the start line, one at half way, and a third coming up the Mall to the finish. Them's the only three cigarettes I smoke all year.

I'm so nervous, I almost ask her for one. I feel sick on the walk from Maze Hill station to the start and I'm unusually withdrawn when I get there. I'm in a tent with the other media runners, but spend much of the final hour locked in a toilet cubicle.

Finally we're called to the start line, where I'm a bundle of nervous energy. I check my watch is working for the eleventh time, then impulsively decide to dispense with my running cap. It's brand new, cost me almost £30 two days ago. In my pre-race flap, I toss it onto the pile of discarded old clothes that runners have been wearing to keep warm.

British astronaut Tim Peake, orbiting the Earth on board the International Space Station, has recorded a good-luck message to start the race, which is relayed via giant screens. He gets such a big cheer, I wonder briefly if he can actually hear it in space. Tim's message ends with a 10-second countdown, the starting gun fires, and suddenly we're on our way to Westminster.

The joy of motion courses through my legs and I become strangely elated. A few yards into the race, I glance to my left and see Danny Mills, the ex-England footballer, scampering alongside. We exchange hellos and he asks what time I'm hoping for.

'Anything starting with a two.'

The words are out of my mouth before I have a chance to think and suddenly it's too late to shove them back in.

There it is then. Having spent months keeping my sub-3 goal a close secret, I've blurted it out within seconds of starting. I've not even told my wife. I've barely admitted it to myself. Not after all the pain and disappointment of many near-misses.

The PB stands unflinchingly at 3:02:11. Despite years of trying, I've been unable to persuade my legs to carry me 26.2 miles any quicker. The quest to take 2 minutes and 12 seconds off my marathon time even began to erode my joy of running. I took to calling my PB of 3:02, a 2:62 … Delusional, I know.

I'd promised myself – and my family – that I'd simply stopped trying. I decided it simply wasn't worth the hassle. Plus, I'd recently fallen in love with fell running, which felt more soulful and spiritual. On roads, chasing a time, your brain's basically buried in your Garmin. On trails, running marathons through forests, over clifftops and in mountains, you're revelling in movement and nature.

But then again, the siren call of the sub-3 marathon. The amateur runner's Holy Grail. Somehow I couldn't let it go. And on a freezing Monday morning just before Christmas, when I found myself jogging past our local running track on the way to the river, I decided on a whim to turn in. And turn myself inside out.

That icy morning was exactly 17 weeks before London, the length of most training plans. And when I'd obsessed about my times before, Monday had been the dreaded 'Yasso' day. A Yasso is two laps of the track, half a mile, run as fast as possible. Ten times. It's an excellent forecaster of your marathon time, but it's bloody hard work. That Monday, I got properly stuck in. Beginning again to wonder *what if …*

Four months later, and suddenly, my secret is out. Saying it out loud to Danny Mills shocks me a little. It seemed safer when only I knew what I was up to.

Mind you, my wife Caroline doubtless had her suspicions. All those times I sneakily ran twice in a day. All the pre-dawn hours spent doing grisly long runs before anyone woke up at weekends. All the painful interval sessions painstakingly added to my running log. All the bloody Yassos …

They've all come down to the next three hours, the next 26 miles.

After the momentary shock of admission, I experience a strange feeling of freedom. I've 'fessed up. The relief seems to spread down into my legs. They're suddenly springy and bouncy. I wish Danny all the best and speed up.

We've started at the front of the field with the rest of the media and celebrity runners, including Jenson Button, Natalie Dormer and marathon stalwarts Sophie Raworth and Chris Evans. Just behind us are the seriously quick club runners. In the early stages they simply stream past. I've made the mistake before of trying to keep up. You feel you're running slowly because you're being overtaken left, right and centre. But having trained and tapered, you're actually running far too fast. Last year, aiming to run the first mile in around 6:45, I was horrified when the watch beeped at 5:55. I knew I'd pay for that later in the race – and did, emphatically. By Mile 20, I was running through quicksand on the Embankment.

I'm determined to be sensible this time. No way am I wasting all that training. This feels like a final throw of the dice.

About four miles in, I see Jules. He's one of the magnificent seven charity auction winners running with us for BBC Children in Need. We only met the previous day, but I know he's an endurance athlete of prodigious ability, fresh from victory in a 400-mile race in the Arctic. I also know he's as keen as I am to break the magic three-hour barrier. I tell him he's running too fast, that there are loud echoes of my own folly on the same streets 12 months earlier. We decide he should synch with my pace and agree to run the next mile or two together.

We end up running the rest of the race together. And becoming firm friends in the process.

I have one of those blissful days when everything works exactly as it should. My Garmin bleeps obediently every time I run under a big arch of red balloons ticking off another mile. My brain stays clear and focused. And most of all, my legs feel invincible.

We go through halfway in 1:27, giving us almost three minutes to play with. For a long time, we don't think we'll need them – Jules and I are flying.

Except, suddenly, when he's not. When he stops five miles from the finish suffering with cramp and implores me to carry on without him. I channel my inner Sir Alex Ferguson and deliver the first and only motivational hairdryer speech of my life.

'YOU WILL NOT GIVE UP HERE,' I shout at Jules. 'You've got one job, one thing to do … Nothing else matters. Nothing else *exists* but the backs of my ankles. Focus on my feet and bloody well keep up!'

I can only guess what agonies Jules goes through to stay with me. I can't see his face because he's behind me. But something about him seems to draw every spectator's eye. Five-deep along the Embankment, the only name they roar is Jules. They must be seeing his tortured expression and realising they're urgently needed. As one, they're reading the name on his vest and shouting encouragement. Wonderfully, it does the trick. Five minutes later, Jules is back alongside me and we're back on track.

No sooner have we started re-counting those sub-3 chickens when we run into Liam. Almost literally.

Liam is another member of our Children in Need brigade and equally anxious for a finishing time starting with a two. He seems to be in the painful throes of the very definition of a 'go hard and hang on' marathon. But he's not hanging on very well, as we discover when we almost crash into the back of him. The stream of runners is surging strongly towards Westminster, yet Liam seems to be going backwards against the tide.

Jules shouts into one ear while I exhort into the other. Between us, we manage to persuade Liam to run with us for as long as he can. Suddenly, with four miles to go, we've become a gang of three, all of us determined to get this done.

And, with minimal further drama, that's exactly what we do.

Running past Buckingham Palace and turning right up the Mall is one of my favourite-ever running moments. My favourite and my best.

We look up at the clock over the finish line and we know it's in the bag. We cross the line in 2:59:14.

Two, fifty-nine, fourteen.

TWO, fifty-nine, fourteen!!!

You shouldn't really stop on the finish line. Politeness dictates that you should keep moving to leave room for those finishing just behind. But the moment means so much that we collapse instinctively into a group hug within a footstep of the timing mat – one of those magical, unforgettable hugs.

In my memory, the hug is filled with joy and elation and we're soaring. In reality, we see a picture of ourselves in the *Telegraph* the following day and we look shattered and bedraggled. Three castaways.

The fact it was a shared experience only adds to the enjoyment, as do all those failures and near-misses along the way.

I'm utterly content. I feel complete. I feel ridiculously grateful.

The marathon has given me so much. It's helped me learn discipline and determination. It's made me fit and strong and many friends. It's taught me about the important things in life. And now it's given me a 2:59.

I almost want to reach across the centuries and thank Pheidippides. He should know what he started with that desperate dash to Athens from Marathon, he should know about his legacy.

Thousands of years on, how do you know if someone has run a marathon?

They will tell you!

PART TWO

HOW ANYONE CAN DO IT

TRAINING

'There are no shortcuts to any place worth going.'
Beverly Sills, soprano

There's nothing fairer than the marathon. Nothing quite as egalitarian. Not in sport, and not in life. Simply this: train hard enough and you'll finish it.

I once went for a leisurely jog with a Dutch TV commentator (and sub-2:30 marathon runner) during the 2008 Beijing Olympics. I've since forgotten his name, but I will always remember what he said as we finished our run back at the Olympic Park. I'd yet to enter any race at that stage, and asked him nervously about training for a marathon. 'Nothing to worry about,' he said. 'Just gradually increase the mileage, starting and ending at your own front door.'

He's right. Often the hardest thing is getting out in the first place. Plus, it really doesn't matter what's behind that front door, a stately home or a bedsit. On the start line you'd rather be a well-trained student in second-hand shoes than a billionaire with all the latest gear who's been too busy to put in the miles. Every time you set out on a training run, you're writing a cheque to your future self – and you'll cash them all on Race Day.

Nobody ever regretted training properly for a marathon. Even the thousands who had their 2020 marathons cancelled at the last minute due to the coronavirus pandemic, none of them wished they'd stayed on the sofa. Chris Hauth is an Olympic swimmer and elite Ironman triathlete who has become one of the USA's top endurance coaches. Many of his athletes were preparing to run the iconic Boston Marathon until it was suddenly cancelled. Chris told the *Rich Roll* podcast what he said to those disappointed runners.

> If you look back at all your training for this day, the cumulative little experiences, the things you overcame, the sacrifices you made and the joy you had, it's way more than one day will deliver. More than these next three, four, or five hours. It's the last six months of cumulative micro-experiences – the joy, smiles, pain, difficulty, hardship, sacrifice, discipline, resilience. That is what accumulates way more than just one day. Sure, the emotions are magnified because it's event day, Race Day. It's the competition and the energy of others and the crowd. But if you think back over the last six months, would you trade your fitness, your strength, your experiences, joy and overcoming, for just one day?
>
> Of course, we want to see it to fruition and find out what we're capable of. But the cumulative experiences of training have shaped us so much more than one day can ever deliver.

The best piece of advice I've ever been given about running marathons is to enjoy – rather than endure, or even resent –

all the training. Not that it's ever easy. But then, that's the point. I try to stay humble and be grateful for each and every mile. Even the pre-dawn ones when it's cold and raining and my legs feel like lead weights. Especially those.

Top athletes talk about the *process over results*. There's no better person to ask about that process than top coach Martin Yelling. He presents the brilliant *Marathon Talk* podcast (with his friend Tom Williams, boss of parkrun) and is the official coach of the Virgin Money London Marathon. He also somehow finds time to run the fast-growing kids' mental health charity, Stormbreak, for which I'm proud to be a trustee.

I caught up with Martin on a sweltering Wednesday afternoon at the end of lockdown. Between us, we were looking after four noisy young children, none of whom care about any of this. But they do run around a lot – what kid doesn't?! – so perhaps one day they may find themselves wondering about running a marathon and need advice like this. All I did was pass on the 10 questions I hear most frequently from people training for their first marathon.

1. IT'S SUCH A DAUNTING PROSPECT. WHERE DO YOU EVEN START TRAINING FOR A MARATHON?

I always think you should start with setting out your aspiration and your time budget. Both of those inform your training. Aspiration is what you want to achieve – what do you want to get out of this marathon? And I always encourage people to be quite specific with that, especially if they've never run a marathon before.

I just want to finish.
I want to run it without stopping.
I want to run it in a particular time.
I want the medal.
I want to do it in fancy dress …

Whatever the aspiration is, it helps us know what we're aiming at.

So, we go, 'Right, okay, we're aiming at that. It's on this date. We know the distance and we know what you want to get out of it.' Those are really important things. And the next key thing is how much budget can you reasonably allocate to this preparation? And with that, I'm thinking under-promise and over-deliver to yourself.

Typically, somebody will say, 'Oh, I can put in loads of time. Loads. And I'm going to run five times a week.' And more often than not, they can't. So what we'll do is refine that back a step.

These are the essentials, aspiration and budget. Because once you've refined those, you can then build the main ingredients of that plan around those two things. But without knowing what you want to achieve and how much time you've got to achieve it, how much allocated time you've got to achieve it, it's really difficult.

The other thing which is a really important player is what you know and what you've done already. So, when you talk about what you want to achieve and how much budget you've got to get there, you have to put it in the context of 'What's your background here?'

From 'I've never run before in my life. And I'm terrified of just getting to the end of the road.'

Through to, 'I only run three times a week and I can cover 10k without stopping.'

Or even, 'I run five times a week and I average 30 miles a week.'

They're really different start points. So, when you're pulling together the marathon training plan, ask these five vital questions. Where am I going? What do I want to achieve? When can I get there? How much can I give to that journey? And where is my start point?

2. HOW DO I STOP LIFE GETTING IN THE WAY OF MY TRAINING?

You don't, is the answer to that. And you can't. And you shouldn't. In almost every single situation, if you think life is getting in the way of your training, it probably is for a reason and you should listen.

Obviously, there's a difference between two extremes:

'I'm too busy, I simply can't get it in.'
And 'I've got this huge pressure point in my life that I need to deal with.'

And they're actually really different. The latter is something like, 'I've got a work deadline.' It won't be there forever, but it's definitely there. 'I've got a sick child. I've got a poorly parent. I'm poorly myself.' 'There's X and Y that need doing.' Those pressure points always come. So, if you try and force them out of a marathon training plan, you'll just end up being really cross with yourself.

The other extreme is you saying you're too busy when actually you're a top-level procrastinator. Do you just need to get out of your door? And of course, whatever comes along, you're always too busy anyway.

You need to understand what's a pressure point that affects your training routine and what isn't. Life does get in the way, but you've got to be adaptable and flexible to understand when to go with those issues and when to push through.

3. WHAT HAPPENS IF I MISS A SESSION?

So, if you miss a session, just carry on where you were. If you're following a plan and you miss a session, you've missed it. It's in the past, carry on.

The only way I ever change that is if that session is a key element of the week. Then your training plan would ideally be flexible enough to accommodate it anyway. For example, you're 10 weeks into a 16-week training plan, you've got a really cool threshold session to do that week, it's got a lot of marathon goal pace in it, and it's really going to test you. It's a big session. You've already been cracking out 10 weeks of miles. You miss the session. But you've hopefully still got flexibility in the week to get it done. If it's what I would call a priority, or a focus, can you be adaptable enough in your week to reschedule it? In which case, reschedule it. But if you can't have that flexibility and it's gone, then it's gone.

So, in my planning, I would be saying to somebody, 'This is a really important session. If you can do one this week, do this one. It's not your five-mile easy run, it's this hideous session from hell that you've got to do, but I'd rather you did it than mess about with another four steady runs.' And that encourages people to be a little bit accountable as well.

So, flexibility is really important, but so is not dwelling on something that you've missed.

4. WHAT HAPPENS IF I MISS A WEEK OR TWO?

Right, let's say you're poorly and you miss a block. Typically, if you're following a specific plan and you miss a single week, I would say to you, 'Pick up where you should be in that plan.' But missing one week is very different to missing two or three. Because then what you have to do is ease your way back into the plan by working backwards where you left off. You could afford to miss a week and simply, you've missed it. But for two or three weeks, your body has gone through reversibility in your training. You've lost some fitness. If you're coming back from an injury or illness, you don't want it to reoccur so you've got to be really careful. Instead you probably have to come back a week before where you left off. You'll need to adjust the volume and the intensity of your training until you're back where you were.

So, for example, if you had a three-week layoff, this is where it gets nasty in a marathon build-up: sometimes it can take two weeks to be back to where you left off. So, you're five weeks off where you started. This is why a plan needs to have flex and be responsive. If it goes, well, you can take a couple of weeks out and pick back up. Sometimes it might go not very well and you have to adjust your goals.

5. SHOULD I JOIN A RUNNING GROUP, OR AM I BETTER OFF TRAINING FOR MY FIRST MARATHON ON MY OWN WITH MY PLAN?

That depends on the group and it depends on you. If you join an experienced group and you bowl up for your first run together and everyone else disappears off up the road, that's probably not the right group for you to be in. If you join a group and everyone's so slow that you don't feel like you're making personal progress in the way in which you want to make it, then that may not be the right group either. So, I would say the big question is what do you want to get out of running with others? If it's training benefit, find the right group. If it's social benefit, similarly find the right group. If you want to run with other people, find the right people to run with.

6. SHOULD I RUN IF I'VE GOT A COLD?

Not hard, if it's a light cold. Not at all, if it's a heavy one.

7. DO I NEED TO RUN 26 MILES IN TRAINING?

It depends who you are. Most people no, some people yes. Most people, first few marathons kind of participant, no.

Serious marathon runner, experienced, got some hard training miles behind you, yes.

8. HOW DO I TRAIN TO GET QUICKER?

Run quicker. It's simple: if you want to run faster, you have to run faster. In training, you have to break it down to give yourself some rest, so structure your training once a week in the form of an interval session and run at a pace which is faster than your target race pace. But give yourself rest so you don't fall off the wagon after the third rep.

9. WHAT IS THE WALL, AND HOW DO I STOP MYSELF HITTING IT?

Okay, so the Wall is an imaginary obstacle in the latter stages of an endurance event that comes about because of low levels of energy or enthusiasm. Typically, it's avoidable through appropriate training, relevant pacing, optimal nutrition and bucketloads of perseverance.

10. WHAT TIPS DO YOU HAVE FOR THE TAPER? HOW LONG SHOULD IT BE, HOW MUCH RUNNING SHOULD I DO IN IT?

The general taper rule is less is best. But that doesn't mean nothing. Nothing makes you feel terrible. But too much, too late is an even bigger mistake. The best taper advice is to avoid too much running the closer the race gets. Instead, as Race Day approaches, run a little cleverer. Drop your volume, drop your intensity so you arrive fresh and ready rather than broken and battered and demotivated about the whole bloody thing.

As I say, doing too much is worse than doing too little. Because do too much, you end up arriving at Race Day tired.

Do too little, you end up arriving on the start line lethargic. You've got to think about what comes with too little. Often, it's boredom, eating and doing odd jobs – 'I'll just knock the shed up, I'll just decorate the hallway.' So, you can feel a little bit of lethargy. And when you feel that lethargy, that's when the paranoia about the race creeps in. You've got to keep yourself busy enough, but not be foolishly busy.

The taper is the point where you have to trust the training you've done. People wobble in the last few weeks because they're uncertain that they've done enough. It's not like prepping for an exam. If you don't do enough, physiologically, your body will not adapt in the last few weeks so any running you do doesn't make any difference. May as well not bother to do it.

It takes at least 10 days for any fitness benefits to come through the body – at least. Often more like three weeks – I typically work on a three-week lag. You're going to be smashing yourself and you won't really feel the benefits until three or four weeks later. Potentially, eight weeks later. If we're talking about improved oxygen distribution to the working muscles, your body's got to grow new mitochondria [cells that generate most of the chemical energy needed to power the body's biochemical reactions]. It's got to grow new blood vessels. Your heart's got to be stronger at pumping oxygen-ated blood around your body so it can pump a greater stroke volume. These things don't happen in 10 minutes, even in 10 days. It takes weeks for your body to really adapt. You can feel some low-level adaptation – 'I feel better.' Great. And you *will* feel better. But to do it properly, you need to give it time.

Which neatly returns us to the initial point about how completely fair this all is. In the marathon, you won't be let down by a lack of skill. You won't be let down by teammates. It doesn't matter how big your house is, how many friends you have, or how funny you are. It's just a dance, you being led by the distance. Put in the time, put in the miles, respect it – and you'll be just fine.

In many ways, the training is everything. Running, racing, life, it's always about the journey rather than the destination. As Dr. Seuss rather wonderfully puts it:

You have brains in your head, and feet in your shoes.
You can steer yourself any direction you choose.

And when things start to happen, don't worry, don't stew.
Just go right along. You'll start happening too.

WHAT TO REMEMBER

- Be realistic about how much time you can commit to training and set your goals accordingly;
- If you want to run faster, you have to run faster;
- If you must miss a session, try to make sure it's an easy one;
- Respect the taper – less is best;
- Yes, the race is the destination, but please be sure to enjoy the journey.

STRETCHING AND INJURY PREVENTION

Tip: Waiting for the train? Cleaning your teeth? Cross-train: glute squeezes, calf raises, every little helps!

Oh, God … stretching.

Look, you know you should do it but you're probably mostly not bothering. And on those rare times when you do stretch, you're probably doing it wrong anyway. I know I am.

Or rather, I was.

Then one day I sat down with one of the UK's top physios, Paul Hobrough. He's treated some of the best athletes on the planet and he is the author of two bestselling books, *Running Free of Injuries* and *The Runner's Expert Guide to Stretching*. For less than the cost of a single visit to see him, Paul's books will all but ensure you never need to. Which would be a shame in a way, because he's a thoroughly nice bloke. And he's absolutely devoted to helping runners achieve their best.

Paul and I were both invited to give talks at one of Steve Cram's famous running camps in Rutland Water. In some free time between plyometrics sessions and the afternoon relay races, we found a quiet corner to chat. The sort of chat that you think will take 15 minutes – get some advice from the expert, go and have a cup of tea – but ends up lasting an hour. Because somehow, and this is some trick to pull off, Paul makes injury prevention interesting.

This was our conversation verbatim. I was fascinated; I hope it helps.

Paul, I loved your first book, *Running Free of Injuries*. I have given it as a gift many times and the people who received it, usually injured runners, to be honest, have always loved it. So, let's talk a little bit about running pain-free because that's obviously the goal for everybody. Mind you, I suppose if everyone did, you wouldn't have a job.

Well, yes, in a way. But the first line in that book is that only 7 per cent of people actually do all the exercises that are given to them by a physio, so I figured I could tell everyone what to do and 93 per cent would still come and see me. In actual fact, having the book, telling people how to avoid injury and how to get better from injury has actually improved my practice significantly, so there's something in the psyche there.

And I guess I'm right in thinking that if everybody had absolutely perfect running gait, if everybody ran like Eliud Kipchoge, then you really wouldn't have a job because we would all be just perfect.

Yeah, I think there's something about running mechanics and I've looked at so many different running gaits. You see the shuffler, you see the person with the really high leg kick at the back, really big knee drive. You see people that are very asymmetrical as they're running, it's almost like a limp. And actually, for the longest time, I thought if you just took everybody's natural running style and just made them much stronger and a bit more flexible, then that would be enough, because I think the body will react and develop and produce strength wherever it can, as long as you give it a graded exercise programme, as long as it's allowed to develop over time. And that's where I would say most people come to me with injuries sustained when they tried to affect that curve dramatically and they've tried to develop too quickly. That's predominantly where injuries strike. And I would also say that in the first two years of someone's running career, that's when I'll see them the most and then they kind of get over this hill.

Is there a sense that the body gets used to the fact that 'Oh, running is what I do now.'

There are some people you do need to intervene with their gait. I mean, it's like the old scene with Phoebe from Friends *running through Central Park. It's dreadful. And so, there's some people where you just need to make these little tiny adjustments. Where I have a problem with some of the classical gait analysts is, you go in as one person, they try and change you to all be like the same running style. And I don't think that fits the human physiology. I think that we need to make nip and tuck tiny little adjustments, and if someone wants to work with you over a protracted 9-, 12-month period, you make small adjustments that they get used to and gradually they improve. Because otherwise, it's too much happening to your body and that can actually cause injury.*

That's so interesting. So we don't all want to run like Eliud Kipchoge?

No.

I once had my gait analysed and changed by Mike at The Running & Movement School, who called me an octopus – limbs in all different directions, a bit Phoebe from *Friends* actually. And he just straight-ened me up a bit. And even though I'm far from perfect, I have a flail-ing right leg still when I get tired, I found a way to run, essentially, free from niggles and injuries. So, it's just a case of personalising it.

Yeah. It should be, in many cases, as personal as your glasses' prescription. It's just perfect for you. Say you take someone who's 35 years old, who just got into running, they've got 35 years of perfecting their walking gait and the way they sit and the way they play golf, and that sort of stuff will all have created this muscular skeletal structure, which then they want to run faster. And where the problem lies is, as you're walking, there's about one and a half times your body weight going through your foot, Newton's Third Law of equal and opposite forces, and when you run, it can be two and a half to three and a half times your body weight going through. So, then what you're trying to do is say, 'Well, where's the drop of oil in the right place to make this just a little bit easier for them?' And maybe keep the flailing arm, if it's counterbalanced in some rotation at the hip, which just needs to happen for right now.

It was famously Kenenisa Bekele with his left arm, which had a kink in it because of the school books he used to carry on his way to and from school every morning, and he didn't want to straighten that out because he kind of liked it because it reminded him of his childhood.

Yeah, and Paula Radcliffe has a bit of a nodding head. I heard they actually tried to get her to stop doing that and she couldn't run as fast. Look at Michael Johnson and how upright he was, which defied convention. And there's a GB sprinter, who will remain nameless, who technically looked like a figure skater – lots of lateral movement. But he'd never been injured in 11 years. And a new team came and told him to start more linear. And he was too injured to compete in his home

Olympics in 2012. So, all these stories are where I form my opinion that we just change it slightly for the better.

Okay, so let's assume we have a non-injured runner listening to this. Me now. What are your top tips to remain uninjured? This is what we call prehab, isn't it?

Yeah, exactly.

So, what should people be doing just as maintenance? This is what nobody does, right? If you're not injured, you just go straight out and you take it for granted.

So, fundamentally, the number one thing is core strength. If you were to jump straight to a plank, for example, that that might be too advanced for most people because you're asking for lots and lots of co-contraction.

There are some good low-level, almost Pilates-based exercises, which really make a difference. So, lying on your back, like you're going to do an old-fashioned sit-up, and you place two fingers on the little bony prominences on the front of your pelvis, come in an inch and down an inch, and your fingers should be on a muscle called transverse abdominis. If you cough, you'll feel those muscles bounce. Then a three-stage process of imagine that you're going to have a wee and then stopping the flow. Then drawing your belly button in slightly, then flattening your lower back slightly, gives you this kind of natural corset. And holding that for 10 seconds, 10 times, will start to develop your core strength. Then you can then turn that into a plank and then you can start to develop that onto some other great exercises.

My favourite exercise is a single leg squat, by miles, because you have to have good core control, your knee has to track up and down over your middle toe, your hips need to remain level, so you're working glutes, you're working your stabilisers, you're working your core. And actually, if you think about it, what running is, over a marathon, it might be 40 to 50,000 single leg squats with a bit of impact. So, if you can start to develop your core, then start working out to the extremities, then you're doing very, very well indeed.

So, some base core work, build it up to be more functional, then go to things like the single leg squat. Then you're onto lunges, basic squats, and don't forget to stretch your hip flexors because they can be one of the leading causes of lower back pain when you're running.

And how often should people do all this stuff? Uninjured people.

I believe very, very strongly that what I would now say is not going to be done, so on one side of the room is where I would like everyone to be–

And nobody is?

And nobody is. Nobody is. And on the other side of the room is where pretty much every runner I've ever met is. If I could drag you closer to the middle, then that would be incredible. Just to stop what you're doing three times a week and do 20 minutes. I would make a strong argument that that person would start to get personal bests in six weeks in most of their distances, all else being well, and they would be going probably 60 to 70 per cent of the way to make themselves injury-free.

Even people like me who've been running plenty?

Especially people like you.

Really?

Yeah. Because you've got to a point where you can run 100 miles and not blink, and then go for a run the next day perhaps. And so, if you were to do some local strengthening work, you inevitably would have a benefit, even if it was half a per cent every stride. You put that into a 100-mile race, it's going to be a very significant difference.

Which brings us onto the thorny issue of stretching.

The Runner's Expert Guide to Stretching *should really be a prequel to* Running Free of Injuries *because this is what you do when you're not injured. So, stretching itself is the guilt complex everyone has. And typically, it's done quite badly. It should be simplicity done very, very well.*

When you run, there's like this sliding mechanism of muscle contraction where, if you can think of two hairbrushes or two combs where the prongs interlink and slide over one another and back out again, that's how muscles contract and relax. And so, over the course of doing your long run, those muscle contractions have been in, out, in, out, in, out countless times. And they've combined onto one another, and therefore, overall, the unit of muscle is shorter.

If you don't then stretch that out, you carry that tension into your next run. And if you allow that to build up over time, and you get lots of muscle knots and trigger points in your muscle, then you're effectively asking a shortened unit to do exactly the same thing that your running technique expects it to be able to do. Therefore, muscle injury or tendon problems can occur. So, the shortest amount of stretching after a run can just restore the optimum length and you're ready for your next session.

So, the key thing is stretch after, not before, a run, yes?

Correct. Yeah.

Which are the key stretches that people should do?

So, the calf muscle is quite a famous one. Sorry for any vegans or vegetarians, but the way I describe it, you've got two chicken fillets, the two main calf muscles. They're sat just on top of a slab of steak, which is the soleus muscle, and the chicken fillet muscles, the ones that you can see through your skin if you look at your calf, they're about the only muscle that goes through its full range of movement when running.

What I don't really like is people suddenly dropping off a step. I think it's a little bit too aggressive after a run. So, you just place your foot against a wall or a tree, lock your leg out, or lock your knee out, and then just push your hips towards the wall or tree and that really helps with stretching.

This is all until you feel the stretch and then until a little bit of pain. Where do you stop?

Yeah, a mild discomfort. Yeah, particularly after running. The point is, you'd be better off having a mild pulling rather than searching for this deep, agonising stretch and holding it for longer.

And if you do do the deep, agonising stretches, are you doing yourself more harm than good?

Potentially. The problem is that after you've run, whether you've run hard or you've run far or both, there is trauma within the muscle. That's how we ultimately build that better. So, what you don't want to do is to put more trauma into the muscle, so a gentle stretch where you prolong the hold so that these cross bridges that have formed can just gently relax and go back to their optimum length.

Five seconds, 10 seconds, 30 seconds?

Thirty. Thirty plus. Yeah.

Per calf?

Yeah. There's about 12 seconds before your brain, your central nervous system, stops resisting the stretch, so you have to at least get past 12 seconds. Otherwise, it's just your brain resisting it.

So, that's the straight leg. That's the chicken fillets. That's for your gastrocnemius. Now, you need to do exactly the same thing, but with your knees slightly bent, then that does the slab of steak, the soleus.

The soleus is the forgotten runner's muscle. Imagine that you're a ski jumper, Eddie the Eagle Edwards, and you land the ski jump so your feet are staggered one forward, one back and both knees are bent.

You would be stretching the rear on your soleus muscle. So, that's a really nice one to do, an important one to do.

Okay, in all the miles I've run, Paul, over the years, all the training runs, all the races, thousands and thousands of miles, would you like to know how many times, in all of that time, I have stretched my soleus muscle?

I'm going to be shocked, am I?

It's none.

It's none? Right, okay.

None. It's actually none. I didn't even know I should do it until just now.

Oh, right. Well, there you go. Look at the growth. I just desperately want people to stretch.

The hip flexor is a huge one. So, people spend all day, pretty much, sitting down in some shape or form. They then go to bed and they sleep in the foetal position. They're putting their hip flexors on this shortened position. Now, the hip flexor runs from the lower back, comes through, almost to the front of the body, and attaches onto the top of your thigh bone. So, your lower back typically is weaker than the hip flexor muscle, so that becomes tight because you're sitting and you're lying in this crook position. And then you bounce up from work, as you do, and get out on your run, having spent a lot of time sitting down with your hip flexor operating at 50 per cent of its length.

And then, if you have a reasonable running style, you then take your hip flexor through to almost its maximum range in a matter of seconds, cold to hot straight away. And so, it's a small wonder that people find their back aching as they go about their run. So, the hip flexor is, if you took a massive stride forwards and then lowered your trailing knee to the floor, you would be in a lunge position. Most people are familiar with the lunge position. Then all you need to do is stand up *tall, push your hips forward and where the trailing knee is on the floor, you just twist slightly away from that. So, if your right knee is on the floor, you twist slightly to the left and you'll feel a pull in the front of that hip.*

And that is stretching the hip flexor muscles, and if you could just gently elongate those after each run, over a course of two or three weeks, I'm almost certain, unless you have something pathologically going on with your lower back, that your lower back will feel freer, will have been less achy, if achy at all, and you actually find yourself running faster.

This is excellent. So, we've got the hip flexors, we've got the calf and the soleus. And then I'm guessing that in between the two needs a bit of stretching, the hamstring and the quads?

Yes, quads and hamstrings need stretching, but there's one muscle that I'd put way ahead of those: the glutes, the bum muscles. They are your main driving force. And actually, when you've got tight hip flexors, you tend to find you've got very underactive glutes. So, your bum muscles, you're sitting on them all day, they become long, they become lazy, and because you've got tight hip flexors from sitting all day, it makes it almost impossible for your glutes to fire and become your main mover. So, by releasing the hip flexors and starting to work on strengthening and stretching out the glutes, you then really start to improve your running.

If you were to lie on your front and bend one knee to 90 degrees, then your foot, if you flattened it, would be perpendicular to the ceiling. Imagine that you put a tray of champagne flutes on top of your foot. It could be Prosecco, we don't mind. Then what you need to try and do is to lift that tray up about an inch and a half, two inches, without spilling any. And if you can do that, you start to work your glute muscle. Because you bent the knees so the hamstring's shortened and weakened, you're clearly working the glute. Then afterwards, if you were to hug your knee close to your body and pull your foot in a little bit, you'd be doing a lovely glute stretch.

If you get your glutes to just fire at the right time, in theory you should run faster. If not, then you're using your hamstrings, which typically are very short and do need stretching. But they're also a weak hip extensor, which means that you're using a muscle that isn't very good at driving you forwards, ahead of one that's brilliant at doing that job.

What about the hamstring and the quad stretch?

Yep. So, one of my bugbears about the way people stretch hamstrings, if you're of a certain age then you are taught at school to either lock your knees out and bend down towards the floor or to have your legs out in front of you and stretch down towards your feet. And frankly, I don't like that type of stretching at all. I think that you need to have a bent knee. You must have a bent knee. Otherwise, what you're doing is stretching the sciatic nerve that goes down the back of the leg. You're better off putting your heel on a chair, having a bent knee, keep a straight back and lean forwards. That will stretch hamstrings. You should feel it in the belly of the muscle, you shouldn't feel it behind the knee.

For the quads, one of the biggest problems is you take hold of your foot and you put it up to your backside and your knee is allowed to track forwards from the straight leg. So, you're not actually stretching the quad, you're just holding onto your heel. So, you really must hold that in your backside and take the knee backwards a little bit as well. But to do it truthfully, lie on your front and pull your heel up to your bum because then you can't do it wrong.

WHAT TO REMEMBER

- Stretch after – not before – a run;
- Each stretch should be 30 seconds-plus;
- Calf, hip flexors and glutes are equally important, probably even more so, than hamstrings and quads.

INJURY

Tip: Beach running strengthens your feet and ankles.

It's a day I'll never forget. Six months or so after I first got into running and I've gone from being unable to make it to the end of my street to entering my first half-marathon. My confidence is growing. Spiralling, you might say.

I go out for a run, heading straight for the river as usual. After half a mile, just as I reach the water and join the Thames towpath opposite Fulham's famous football ground, Craven Cottage, the outside of my left knee starts grating. It's painful, but this has happened before so I don't fret unduly. I know that within five minutes or so the pain will recede and I'll continue merrily along my way down the river.

Only this time, the pain doesn't go away. I wait patiently, running slower, giving it every chance. But instead of receding like it always has done, it swells somewhat alarmingly. I stop and rub the offending knee. Start running again. But the outside of the knee keeps grinding away, more than annoying now. This is proper pain. I stop, unsure what to do.

Is this what an injury feels like?

I limp home disconsolately. A local physio diagnoses runner's knee, or iliotibial band syndrome (ITBS). It's an overuse injury of the tissues on the outer part of thigh that connect the knee with the hip. He advises strengthening exercises and a lengthy rest from running.

I don't like the physio's diagnosis and go to see a top sports doctor. Simon Kemp puts the world's best rugby players back together ... Surely he'll have a magic bullet for an amateur runner's hurty left knee? He doesn't. Instead he sets me on the road to rest and rehab with some wise words about running too much, too quickly. Many people could easily manage a half-marathon within six months of starting to run but not, it seems, me.

The rule of thumb is to increase training time and volume by no more than 10 per cent every week. So, if you ran 10 miles last week, with your longest run being five, then this week, you shouldn't do more than 11 miles in total, with your long run being a maximum of five and a half miles.

It's helpful to categorise runners into red, amber or green risk categories. Both their initial running loads and first running goal need to be proportionate to where they are starting from. And really, the approach for each of these three groups needs to be different.

Green is: I've always been a regular runner. I may have lapsed for a little while, but I ran at school and/or university and I haven't had long periods of not running.

Amber is: I've run on and off, I've done other sports, I've remained fit and active. Maybe I've not been running that much recently but I've been doing running-related activities – football, tennis, hockey, etc. regularly.

Red is: I don't have any significant previous regular running experience. I may be heavy. Any exercise that I've done recently has been on a bike (limited weight-bearing) or in the swimming pool. I may have had previous problems when I have run, I may know that I have knee pain, hip pain. I may have had previous lower limb surgery. I may have had a previous fracture to the leg or ankle.

Whilst the Green group might start training for a marathon, the Red group needs to set more realistic goals – possibly 5km or 10km rather than a half-marathon and start running less often each week, at a slower pace for less time until they develop the robustness they need to increase the amount they run. They can get there but they need to take it more slowly than the Green group and allow more time for recovery between runs. They may well benefit from some non-running based training – cycling, swimming or an elliptical trainer (also known as a cross-trainer) in the gym – to help them become more robust.

Our five-year-old daughter Mary has four 'D-words' which have been banned in her classroom and consequently in our home: idiot, bad, stupid and (curiously) hate. Well, I hated every stupid minute I couldn't run. I'd be driving along, seeing people out jogging, and think bad thoughts. Especially if the idiots didn't look grateful. And I know it's hard to look grateful while running, but still.

I followed medical advice, rested, did my rehab exercises and returned to running after a few frustrating weeks, via two experts on gait analysis, Mike Antoniades at The Running & Movement School in London, and Dr Jessica Bruce, world record holder for a marathon pushing a buggy and founder of Run3D in Oxford. Both told me in no uncertain terms that I urgently needed to change the way I run to avoid repeat injuries.

As Mike put it when I returned to his school to talk to him, several injury-free years (and marathons) later:

> I categorise runners – bad runners – into four groups. The Thumpers hit the ground really hard. The Shufflers barely lift their feet. The Slows could walk faster than they run – you often see them in the park at weekends. And you were an Octopus: arms and legs all over the place.
>
> Humans are cross-lateral animals, so when we move the left leg, we also move the right arm. That's the way we were designed. If you haven't been taught that, and you don't have the background of skills, then you just run how you think is normal. And in some cases, and you were one of them, it's as if you've got four independent limbs going in four completely different directions.

I learned to pump my arms whenever I was struggling during a long run and could feel my technique (such as it is) flagging. And somehow that seemed to act as a trigger for everything to come together and I continued largely pain-free.

But then I ignored the mounting pain during the marathon at the end of my first, somewhat shambolic, Ironman triathlon. As the miles ticked by, I could literally feel the damage I was doing to my left knee. I refused to stop, but eight years on, that knee still hurts most days. Really quite badly if I jar or twist it, and it often swells alarmingly during a hard run. Was it worth it? Probably not. Would I refuse to stop again today? Probably.

Before I tell you this next bit, please take heed of the rest of this paragraph. When injured, you may well need to seek professional advice, particularly in the early days or if you start changing up your mileage or terrain. Sometimes rest and rehab are the best way back to where you were. However I also believe you can learn to listen to your body's aches and twinges and evaluate them for yourself.

I've now assumed a self-taught, laid-back attitude to injuries; I reckon that for the most part, the body will find a way to cope. If it's true that we were once persistent hunters who relied on running long distances for our food, surely we couldn't be stopped by the odd hip sprain or muscle tear? Our bodies would have had to find a way to carry on, or we'd have starved. 'Stop moaning and get on with it' is basically the approach I adopt whenever I get a niggle and it's largely worked.

But then again, I've been pretty lucky of late. And the one time I tried to force an injured ankle around a five-day mountain race in Wales, I failed entirely.

I also occasionally employ a trick I heard from a fellow endurance runner. This definitely comes under the 'do not try this at home' umbrella, but it's worked for me. When I'm in pain during a race, the injury sort of pain rather than the exhaustion sort, instead of trying not to think about it, I do the exact opposite. I dial right down into the pain. Give it the freedom of my mind. Let it blossom. Let the toddler have the tantrum. Because the thing is, tantrums blow themselves out eventually. The pain does swell, intensify and then suddenly disappears. The theory being, there's only a certain amount of information the nerve endings can send to the brain, after which they become overloaded and just sort of give up.

I'm keen to put my theory to a professional. Fortunately, top physio Paul Hobrough, who helped us out with his stretching advice, is no stranger to running loonies like me:

> Pain science is this huge growth area – our increasing understanding of how the brain rationalises pain. If you don't have a brain, you cannot feel pain. If I sprain my ankle, there's a message that goes to my brain, which effectively is 25 per cent of the actual pain that I will feel. It's a stimulus.
>
> Your brain gets this message, which is purely, 'Something has happened at the ankle. We don't know what, but we think it might be bad.' Your brain then goes, 'Okay, what information have I got about the ankle? What have I read? What have I learned? What experience do I have of that?' It draws together all this information. And perhaps you have a race in a week's time, so your brain is also going, 'This is really bad,' or, 'You've had this before and you were out for eight weeks.' All that information comes together, the sensation of pain, the added 75 per cent, and then makes it so horrific you can't walk on the ankle.
>
> What you're doing when you're running is you are controlling the pain. You're focusing on it and you're saying, 'Give me everything you've got. I don't care. I'm going to still run.' Your brain gets credible evidence that all of your toes aren't about to drop off and it goes, 'Maybe we've got this wrong,' and it down-regulates the signal. It's a very, very important point of what physio does, to help people to understand what their pain actually means.

Which is all very well for the experienced runner. But running-related pain when you're just starting can be terrifying. The week before my first marathon in Barcelona, I had a classic case of maranoia. I was in such pain, all of it psychosomatic, that I basically ruined a family weekend break. In the months leading up to the big spring marathons, always the busiest time for a running physio, up to 50 per cent of Paul's clients are newish runners with painful knees. How are they meant to know whether they should be worried or not?

What we try and do with pain science is to educate people that pain is not equal to damage, and damage does not mean pain. Some people even say, 'The minute I rang up and booked the physio appointment, my pain seemed less,' because you're doing something about it. What we try and do is to help people to understand what is a normal reaction to pain and what are the things that they can perhaps start to control.

For example, I had a lady in who couldn't sleep at night because of the pain in her hip, but all through the day she was pain-free. What I said to her was, 'All through the day, you're busy. Your brain's busy. It's not thinking about it. You've now associated going to bed as being painful. Your brain is, "Oh we're getting into bed, are we? Okay, it's going to be really painful. I'm going to stop you sleeping."'

I actually flipped it around and said to her, 'You know how a scab might itch when it's repairing? That pain you're feeling is the same. Your body's fixing itself whilst you're in bed and that is a good thing.' She texted me the next day and went, 'I've had my first good night's sleep in ages,' because it's just about flipping it into a different reference point.

I've yet to meet the runner who enjoys being injured on any level. When you fall in love with running, especially as hard as I have, being unable to get out there seems like torture.

I've had both sorts of runner's knee. Iliotibial band syndrome, that first-ever running injury that reared its head on the Thames towpath opposite Fulham FC, and also mis-tracking of the kneecap. The patella is smooth and round on the front, a giant chocolate button, but the underside is like a stubby shark's fin which lets it track in the thigh bone. When that starts flailing left and right, perhaps because of foot position or hip weakness, that's also called runner's knee. Paul, of course, has just the exercise to help prevent it:

The single-leg squat. Standing on one leg and bending your knee up and down and keeping the knee over your middle toe, not going beyond it, but centrally over the middle toe and keeping your hips square. It's a great way of building up functionally the strength you need to maintain that knee alignment.

Shin splints are another common injury that can stop us in our tracks. Unless, apparently, we're happy to do some hill work:

With shin splints, it's okay to do a bit of running on a gradient, typically on a treadmill. The problem is, the muscles that lower the foot down under control get too tired. They become too short to do the job, so you start flapping your feet down like a duck.

Whilst I'm treating you, if I put the immediate front portion of the path slightly higher for you, then you've got enough strength to drop to that 30-degree angle, say. But under no circumstances do you run on the flat and absolutely not running downhill, whilst we're getting you better from shin splints.

Work our way down the leg then. The lower an injury strikes, the more it'll stop you in your tracks.

When you hurt an ankle, it tends to be one of the few acute (rather than chronic) injuries. With acute injuries, you know the time, the day and exactly where you were, what you were wearing when it happened. A chronic injury builds up over time until you can't run anymore.

There are three different types of acute ankle injuries. Grade 1 is a small nick in the ligament. Grade 2, which is a larger tear, is more painful and the foot may feel wobbly. With Grade 3, the ligament is completely torn.

We need to support the ankle first because a Grade 1 very quickly can become a Grade 2, a Grade 2 can quite easily become a Grade 3.

Just released from Germany is an ankle support with artificial intelligence in it that acts like a seatbelt. You get perfect freedom of movement. If the velocity of the sprain is such, then this will kick in and this is just going to revolutionise the way we treat ankles.

Finally, to the underside of your foot. The plantar fascia is a thick, web-like ligament that connects your heel to your toes. It acts as a shock absorber and supports the arch of your foot, helping you walk. Plantar fasciitis, pain on the bottom of your foot, is horrible. The first time I experienced the so-called Geordie injury (just try saying plantar fasciitis in a north-east accent), it seemed to grow out of a frozen pea.

I got out of bed one morning and there it was, a discomfort like stepping on a frozen pea. Two or three steps later, it went away. The next morning, it took four steps before disappearing. Then several weeks later, I could feel it while walking around all morning, but I still wasn't bothered. I could still run, that was the main thing. But that was also my big mistake. Because soon, it hurt too much to run and took weeks to recover from.

> It's one of those things that the more you keep doing on it, the worse it gets and the far, far harder it is for us to repair. The first thing we need to do is get people writing the alphabet with their foot in mid-air to get some warmth and blood to the area. Then we get them to step into quite cushioned and quite supportive footwear. Then we get them doing a number of stretches six times a day, pulling the toes back towards the shin. And you can actually wear something called a Strassburg Sock overnight, which keeps your foot in this extended position to help the repair.

Injuries are the worst thing about running, no question. The chronic ones, which is to say the usual ones, happen because our muscles are too weak or too short to do their job. If we rest, they won't be lengthening or strengthening.

And paradoxically, that's actually good news. It means these days we can generally keep running during treatment. Just see a physio who understands that most runners largely ignore advice to stop running anyway.

WHAT TO REMEMBER

- You tend to get injured much more during the first two years of running, while your body's getting used to the idea that you're a runner now;
- Increase total training time and distance by no more than 10 per cent a week;
- The single leg squat is the single best exercise to improve leg and knee stability, just make sure your knee doesn't collapse inwards;
- Try to learn the difference between a niggle and an injury;
- If in doubt, see a physio – the sooner you do, the quicker you'll be back running.

MENTAL STRENGTH

Tip: Smiling whilst running really helps! It gives better economy, makes you feel more relaxed. In contrast, frowning may increase tension and make your run feel harder.

October 2019 and Kenenisa Bekele is running through the Brandenburg Gate. He's about to complete a remarkable comeback to marathon running at the age of 37 and win the Berlin Marathon for the second time. But more than that, he's giving everything he has to break the world record. The clock above the finish line ticks over relentlessly. Commentators shout excitedly into microphones. Thousands around the finish area will him on. This is going to be mighty close … One final, lung-bursting surge forwards and the great Ethiopian crosses the line in 2:01:41.

He's missed out by two seconds.

Two seconds over 26.2 miles and 122 minutes. Two seconds faster and he'd have also earned a €50,000 bonus.

Bekele won gold medals galore and set longstanding world records on the track. But something about the marathon world record, the Big One, seems to slip through his fingers.

Three years previously in Berlin, Bekele won the race in 2:03:03, missing out on the then-world record by six seconds.

Further back down the field in 2019, six runners from as far afield as Moldova, Poland and New Zealand all fail to break the magical three-hour barrier by one second or less. And then six runners, including a Brazilian and a Taiwanese, were within a second of breaking five hours.

Next stop, Monza Formula 1 track in Italy, where Eliud Kipchoge is busting a gut to become the first person to run a marathon in under two hours. He couldn't be working any harder; this is the culmination of six months' painstaking training and millions of dollars of investment. And yet those phenomenal legs of his just can't keep up with the required pace and he comes home, disappointingly, in 2:00:25. One second quicker per mile would've done it.

In all of the above cases, you're bound to wonder, *what if*? Kipchoge and Bekele rocketing along at just over four and a half minutes per mile, and those five-hour runners at 11 minutes plus, they were all giving it everything, surely? When a world record is on the line. And when you've travelled as far as those unfortunate three- and five-hour finishers, thousands of miles just to run in Berlin, it must be heartbreaking to miss your goal by a second or less. Some say that a marathon 'counts', it's proper, if it's run in under five hours. To keen amateurs and club runners, a sub-three finish is the Holy Grail. As for a world record or the first-ever sub-2, athletics immortality.

So, Bekele and Kipchoge, the three-hour brigade from Moldova, Poland and New Zealand, and two hours later, the Brazilian and the Taiwanese, straining every sinew, pushing through the pain, on the cliff edge of their physical limits, watching the finish line clock tick agonisingly over, they must have felt that it was absolutely beyond their control. That they were all running as fast as they possibly could and that's the end of it.

But were they?

Take the 1996 men's Olympic marathon, the closest-ever finish. Three seconds separated the gold and silver medallists. In second place, Lee Bong-ju of South Korea. Did he *really* give everything? You'd imagine he did, so close to history and glory. If ever there was a situation to run yourself into a coma, this was it.

Yet when he lost, Lee then somehow found the energy to pick up his national flag and start jogging around the track, taking in the cheers of a rapt crowd. Therefore, during the race itself, he clearly wasn't able to run himself to a point where his muscles truly couldn't move anymore. Why?

Alex Hutchinson is a former athlete-turned-journalist. During his early career he struggled to run a mile in under four minutes. He'd keep missing out by the odd second. Then during one inauspicious race when he was simply feeling his way back from injury, he asked a friend to call out his lap times each time he went past: eight laps of an indoor track.

The first time he came past, the friend misread the watch and called out 27 seconds when the real time was 33. Suddenly, Alex was three seconds ahead of four-minute mile pace and without even trying that hard. Suddenly there was a spring in his step, a new self-belief. The following laps went by in a blur of speed and exhilaration, and that four-minute barrier which had always seemed beyond him was broken emphatically. It got him thinking about how much the mind arbitrates our physical limits.

Many years of research later, often using himself as his own lab rat and speaking to the leading experts in the field, Alex published one of my favourite books on sport, *Endure: Mind, Body and the Curiously Elastic Limits of Human Performance*.

Whenever I need guidance in this field, I give him a call. And he's still very good about answering his phone to me, given that he lives in Canada and it's generally the middle of the night when it rings.

So, let's say you're running a marathon, you're trying to stay with one of the pacers, they pull away from you and you're like, 'Oh, well, I wish I could go with them, but I'm doing everything I can and they're just faster than me.' And then you turn the corner and you see the finish line in the distance and all of a sudden, you're sprinting.

And this is something that's happened to me more times than I care to admit. And we accept that as natural because almost everyone has that feeling. But when you stop and think about it, clearly what felt like a non-negotiable limit was actually somehow negotiable.

The book sprang from a frustration that I would finish races thinking, why on earth didn't I go a little faster in the middle? I mean, because I know from the end, when I sprinted, that I had more energy. But by the time I finished the book, I'm not sure I would still call it a frustration. It's actually one of the great things about endurance. I mean, I think it would be boring to watch races and to participate in races if you always knew exactly how fast you'd be able to run. One of the great things about the sport is how elastic those limits are and how you can surprise yourself on a good day.

There are many stories of course of how people perform extraordinary, seemingly impossible athletic feats in emergencies. Most often cited is the baby under the car which the mother lifts with one hand. In a panic situation, in life or death, people find there is more in their muscles.

A scientist named Tim Noakes, who's been highly influential in exploring the limits of endurance, tells the 1996 Olympic Marathon story during his talks. He shows footage of the silver medallist finishing three seconds behind the winner, then bouncing around on his victory lap with the South Korean flag draped around his shoulders. If you follow the path of elastic limits to its logical conclusion, then it can't be our muscles stopping us from reaching our full potential. It must be our brain. And the obvious question is, can we train our brain? Alex has tried.

There's been some fascinating research, a bunch of it funded by the UK Ministry of Defence, trying to investigate computer-based training to enhance brain endurance. And I tried it for 12 weeks before the marathon, spending up to an hour a day, five days a week, sitting in front of a computer, tapping the buttons in response to what was happening on the screen. This was pushing my ability to sustain concentration, keep my finger as close as possible to the flame, as it were. And the end result? I discovered that brain endurance training is absolutely miserable and time-consuming and I would never want to do it again. But maybe if there was Olympic gold on the line, I would consider it. But I think, to me, the best answer for training your brain is not to sit in front of the computer, it's to get outside and just run a little more because that trains your brain too.

It's also a good idea of course to consider how you'll deal with the mental pressures on the start line.

The hours and minutes leading up to a marathon are my favourite place in all of sport. All that nervous energy and excitement, if only you could bottle it or take it as a supplement.

Trouble is, some people get so nervous and worked up, they can ruin their race before it even begins. I'm a big talker at the start of any race – occasionally slipping into the realms of over-talking if I'm honest, sorry to anyone I've annoyed. But what I've gleaned from all those chats before all those big races is a bucketload of tips on how to tame those butterflies. So here goes, five fantastic tips I've copied from others to calm start-line nerves.

FOCUS ON SOMEONE OR SOMETHING ELSE

Helping someone else through their pre-race nerves will necessarily mean you feel calmer about your own. And I once met a couple who distract themselves by counting as many different running club vests as they can spot milling about before the start – and compare scores. Their record was 24, but I'm confident we could beat it.

VISUALISATION

Look back on your training. Think of all the people who've helped you along the way. The next 26.2 miles are a representation of all that combined effort and commitment.

And look ahead to your race. Imagine each part of the marathon – and manifest your ultimate success. Have clear intentions of what you want from the next 26.2 miles, feel it and believe it.

REPEAT YOUR MANTRA

This is often cited as something to do when the going gets tough late on, but many people prefer to do this to calm themselves before the storm. Anything from positive affirmation, *'You've got this!'*, *'Stay Strong!'* to something more personal, *'This is for grandma'*. Just find something short that feels right.

A LITTLE NOTE

Everyone has a different reason for signing up for a marathon. Maybe something personal, perhaps a cause, possibly a loved one. Even all three. Coaches frequently suggest that their runners write down the names or reasons on a small piece of paper the night before the race and tuck it in a sock or pocket. It can help focus the mind before the start. And when the distance starts to sting, it can feel like you're literally carrying – or being carried by – those reasons towards the finish.

ONE THING AT A TIME

I once met someone called Joey on the start line in New York – honestly – and his trick was to 'channel my inner

Chandler'. You may remember the one where Monica and Chandler got married. Chandler stopped himself panicking about the enormity of what he was doing by focusing on the little things. Just get dressed, just get a cab to the church, just stand at the front ... Similarly, on the start line on Staten Island, Joey gave his whole focus to tying shoelaces, the queue for the loo, finding the right starting pen. Before he knew it, he was away and running over the Verrazzano-Narrows Bridge.

Once you're running, it's rarely the legs or the lungs that give up first during a marathon, not if you're properly trained. It's the brain. However, just as you can cajole rebelling quad muscles to redouble their efforts, so you can trick your brain into giving you more. For instance, there's new research, which Alex cites in *Endure*, proving that simply swilling a sports drink around your mouth then spitting it out – ingesting none – can boost performance as much as drinking all its vital fuel and electrolytes. I call him yet again to ask him about it.

> Your brain is holding you back during any sort of marathon or endurance performance. It's trying to prevent you from doing too much too soon, and if it thinks there's more fuel on the way, it'll say, 'Oh, okay. I guess we don't need to be quite so cautious.' So you get this mix of brain and body. And if you watch elite marathoners these days, late in the race when their stomachs are getting fed up of trying to deal with sports drink, they'll just take a big mouthful and then spit it out in a big arc across the road.

And what about those runners in Berlin? The woman who travelled all the way from New Zealand, only to fall a second short of breaking three hours? And the Brazilian man who just failed to come in under five? Is there a case of 'if you think you can, you probably can' – and they both probably thought they couldn't?

I would call myself a late and partial convert to that point of view. I think the second half of that statement is the one that's really true. Of course there are physical requirements to do something, but until you believe you can achieve it, it's not possible.

So what can we do, practically, to help us push through whatever barrier we've set for ourselves?

First of all, just to become aware of your internal monologue, what you're thinking about during the hard part of a run, because if you're like me, you'll discover that a lot of the thoughts flashing through your head are things like: 'This sucks.' 'I can't maintain this pace.' 'Why do I do this?' 'How did I let my friend drag me into this?' And that is not helpful at all.

Once you think you can't do it, you're not going to be able to do it. So being aware of what you're saying to yourself gives you the best opportunity to start refusing those negative thoughts and replacing them with something more positive, like yeah, this hurts, but I'm ready for this. And if it's hard, that's because I'm doing it right, and I can push through this, and I can make it, and I can do this.

Annoyingly, it seems there's no magic bullet when it comes to thinking our way to a faster race. But that's actually what makes this fun: the process of pushing back limits gradually. That, and the mystery about to unfold every time you toe the start line of a marathon.

WHAT TO REMEMBER

- Be aware of your inner monologue, replace negative thoughts with positive ones;
- You've almost always got more in your muscles than your brain is letting on;
- Unless you believe you can, you probably can't.

MUSIC

Tip: To help measure intensity level, singing becomes difficult with moderate exercise, talk is hard at high intensity.

I have a guilty secret. I wrote two books about running and named them both after songs. (That's not it). In *Don't Stop Me Now*, every chapter name was a running song, one of my favourites. But by the time the book came out, I'd fallen out of love with my running playlist. I never ran with music. That's the secret. I'd begun to wonder whether music sullied the purity of the running experience. And yes, I do know how pompous that sounds ...

I used to love it. Everything from 'Run Run Run' by The Who to Bruce Springsteen's 'Born to Run'. I was also partial to a bit of cheesy, happy music while running, stuff like Wham!'s 'Wake Me Up Before You Go-Go' or The Vapors' 'Turning Japanese'. It just made me run happy. Eminem's 'Lose Yourself' was my go-to favourite – almost impossible not to up the pace when that came on.

Then there was an embarrassing incident near home. Running on a crowded springtime towpath, I inadvertently blurted out the lyrics to the song currently thumping through my earphones. Just the six-word chorus. An elderly couple I was running past got the full force of my random outburst: '*I'm sexy and I know it.*' They almost certainly didn't know the song and must've thought I was getting something off my narcissistic chest. The shame put me off music and running a bit. That, and the fact I felt like I couldn't properly connect with the running experience if I had music blaring. Again, I do know how that comes across.

But recently, when the mood takes me, I sometimes find myself reaching for the iPod and rocking along the towpath once again. Maybe there's something magical about running to the beat after all.

Costas Karageorghis grew up in a colourful enclave of South London called Brixton. There was a secondhand record store immediately below the family flat. Each morning, rather than being woken by the sweet sound of birdsong, or the sun breaking gently through the net curtains, a thundering base would jolt him out of bed. He'd wipe his sleepy eyes, look out of the window and notice that as people came within earshot of the music, it would change their physiognomy; it put a spring in their step.

So, from a very young age, he became fascinated by how music influenced the human psyche. Fast forward a few decades and he's now professor in sport and exercise psychology at Brunel University, the world's leading expert on music and running. He's also written the definitive book on the subject, *Applying Music in Exercise and Sport*. In it, he states: 'Listening to music is a type of legal performance-enhancing drug. But unlike banned substances in sport, which are often mainly linked to elite athletes, music is a massive game-changer for the masses.'

I'm thrilled Costas finds a window to chat to me in his ludicrously busy diary. I'm sandwiched between a lengthy meeting he's chairing and another he's rushing off to. He purposely brings the former to a prompt finish and rushes back to his office for our chat. We're only interrupted once by a knock on the door. I sense that's miraculously quiet for him, so I get straight to the point and ask him about his copious research.

> Particularly in the last decade or so, we've really been able to take an under-the-bonnet look at how music influences the brain and to fully understand how music changes our behaviour, how the mechanisms bring about those changes in mood, in attitude and even in motor performance.

I've always wondered why people who'll tell you they detest running and couldn't run a step will gaily dance around energetically for two hours without seeming to tire. In a way, is that proof of what Costas is saying?

> Well, from a practical perspective, you've struck the nail on the head. Since the very earliest societies, people have congregated and moved in time to music. In the Maori culture, the word for music and dance is the same. And so this is something that's embedded deep within our DNA. It is of course germane to human procreation and finding a mate. Psychologically, we derive great pleasure from moving in time with music in the presence of others. There's a phenomenon known as shared affective motion experience and there's a whole theory around how we mimic each other's movement patterns.
>
> Interestingly, it would seem that a tempo of around 120 beats per minute seems to be the magic tempo that lures people onto a dance

floor. Also, funnily enough, this is the value of twice the resting heart rate and it's also the rate at which we walk spontaneously. So it seems that this tempo of 120 beats per minute is fused deeply within the human psyche.

But there seems to be a ceiling at around 140 beats per minute. So there's a sweet tempo spot of 120 to 140 beats per minute. We don't seem to derive greater benefit beyond 140 beats per minute. If we want to consciously synchronise our movements to music, then of course we need to select the tempo with the desired movement rates in mind.

The natural next question, for an obsessive runner like me, is about using music to break my marathon PB. Is it as simple as finding the right song? Could Paula Radcliffe have run faster with her favourite tunes in her ears?

Not quite. If you're an elite marathon runner and working at quite a high percentage of your aerobic capacity, it could be that music is an unwanted distraction because those elite athletes focus inwardly on regulating their movement, the function of their organs, their technique.

It tends to work best at low to moderate intensities of exercise or running. And so for Joe and Josephine Public, it could be a great antidote. It could assuage the pain or the unpleasant feelings associated with running or exercise. But also, we know through our research that music can extend your endurance, it can make you run faster, and it can also make you run with greater efficiency. You need to expend fewer calories when running in time with music versus running without music so there are a number of benefits that we've been able to assess and measure.

So if you like, music is preventing some of that fatigue-related communication from taking place in the brain. It also seems to be inhibiting some of the fatigue-related signals that emanate from the musculature and working organs, and it inhibits the processing centrally. It makes us feel as though we're working less hard, as you suggested in your dance example earlier.

But also, if the music is well-selected with our musical predilections, our cultural background, and age group influences in mind, it can elevate our mood, it can enhance positive aspects of mood such as vigour and happiness. And it can reduce negative aspects of mood such as tension, depression, anger, fatigue and confusion.

One of my favourite-ever runs took place one still, summer Sunday morning on West Sands in St Andrews. It's the beach used in the classic film, *Chariots of Fire*. I was up before the lark and had the entire expanse to myself. This was in the days when I religiously ran to music and to complete the athletic perfection, I had Vangelis playing with my ears. The theme tune. In my mind, I was suddenly in the film, part of that happy group of white-vested 1920s Olympians splashing through the shallows: young, fit, glorying in the act of running.

Costas used to be a sprinter. He couldn't of course use music while competing. But pre-competition, he'd also use Vangelis's 'Chariots of Fire' to conjure the right sort of imagery to psych himself up, focus and create a mindset associated with sprinting success. But is there a particular song he'd recommend for a marathon runner hoping to better their time?

Well, one person's music is another person's noise. And it's never a case of one-size-fits-all in terms of applying music, there are great variations from individual to individual. But if we're talking about running-themed tunes, you could warm up with something like 'Running on Sunshine' by Jesus Jackson, that has a tempo of 100 bpm, which would be ideal. If you wanted a tune for low-intensity running, you might use 'Running with the Night' by Lionel Richie, that has a bpm of 120. As you go a little bit faster, say a moderate-intensity run, you might use 'Run to You' by Bryan Adams, it's a rock tune with a tempo of 126. And if you're going at a high-intensity, let's say your heart rate is around 160, 170 bpm, you might use a tune such as 'Born to Run' by Bruce Springsteen, with a bpm of 148.

And what a perfect way to leave a conversation on music and running, with one of the best running songs of all time. Now, where's that iPod?

WHAT TO REMEMBER

- The right song with inspirational lyrics will focus the mind and calm the nerves on the start line;
- Music inhibits fatigue-related signals and helps running feel easier;
- The magic tempo is 120 to 140 beats per minute (bpm).

GADGETS AND GEAR

Tip: Find a running buddy. When the mornings get colder and darker, or if you're apprehensive about starting a training programme, a proven way to stay motivated is to find someone to join you on your training runs.

As you might imagine, *Runner's World* are sent a LOT of running gear. Visit their swanky new offices in Leicester Square and the first thing you notice (after a long time trying and failing to get the lifts to work – there aren't any buttons! – eventually giving up and taking stairs) is an entire wall of running shoes.

An actual wall of shoes.

Rick Pearson is senior editor responsible for some of the magazine's quirkier features. He once persuaded me to meet him in the middle of a pitch-dark, deserted Richmond Park at 2.45 a.m. on a Saturday and then run 10 miles to a terraced, residential street in Hounslow. It was part of a race he'd dreamt up called the 'London Peaks Relay'. A gang of us spent 24 hours carrying a baton to the highest point in every London borough, scaling the heady heights of Hammersmith and Fulham, Camden and the top of Tower Hamlets, fully 16 metres above sea level. Safe to say no oxygen was needed. The final 'peak' was a pub in Westminster. We got there just as it was closing.

Rick also presents the *Runner's World* podcast and tests much of the dizzying array of new gadgets and gear that come to the market on a seemingly endless basis.

It's a Monday mid-morning when we sit down over a cup of tea at *RW* HQ to chat about some of the latest innovations and his recommendations.

Yeah, so we do get a fair amount of gear coming in to *Runner's World* and that one wall is just floor-to-ceiling trainers. It's all organised into brands. But not alphabetical order, we're not that OCD.

Then we have lots of large plastic buckets: one for shorts, one's for socks, one's tee shirts, one's miscellaneous stuff, one's recovery products. So yeah, it's a little bit like walking into a slightly pokey version of Foot Locker.

In my formative running days, I found all the equipment available quite intimidating. I was so dazzled by the advertising efforts of the manufacturers, most weeks I'd emerge from a running shop armed with another must-have accessory.

I discovered I was living in a golden age of the runner. Back in the eighties, when people went out of a jog, all you needed was a tracksuit – accessorised, perhaps, with a headband and matching sweatbands. The only piece of tech was a Sony Walkman to keep you moving to the beat of 'Eye of the

Tiger'. But 'jogging' has transformed into the more serious pursuit of 'running' and there's endless kit to be had.

For me, the tech crept into my life by increments. It started with the quest for the perfect pair of shoes. Then came the base layers – top and tights – that promised to be 'injury-reducing, temperature-controlling and moisture-managing'. Clearly, these were completely vital. They were also £90-a-pop, but hey, I'd get added value with each run. Next, socks. Another £40, but that's money well spent when you consider that the ones I chose were, according to the blurb, 'the result of tireless research work, and the subject of a doctoral thesis'.

Sure, I was setting myself tougher and tougher running goals, but did I really need a hydration backpack to help me achieve them? Or wicking gloves and a £400 GPS watch?

Cycling, fishing, golf … certain sports come with a love of equipment as standard, but running's meant to be simpler, isn't it? The purest form of exercise. Just lace up your shoes and get out there. When Pheidippides made that dash from Marathon to Athens, he probably wasn't wearing hi-vis compression tights.

Rick agrees to go through item by item. First, base layers. They're used for warmth or compression – and often both.

It's probably worth having one or two base layers. But one thing about base layers, they can really start to smell, so merino wool is particularly good because it doesn't hold smell.

With a merino wool base layer, you could actually go running in it, feasibly, then dry it and run in it again – you don't have to keep putting it through the wash. Though you should wash kit fairly regularly, obviously.

It's a warmth thing, but 'dress for the second mile'. Dress thinking that you're going to warm up quickly. Especially here in the UK, I don't think there are many conditions for which you need to wear a running hat or gloves.

Compression's one of these slightly dubious areas. There's evidence to suggest that compression after exercise can speed up recovery. But most people use compression during exercise, and often some of these runs will only be half an hour or so – I'm not sure you really need compression for that kind of outing.

And then for blokes, there's the leggings debate. There's a certain kind of guy who thinks it's kind of weak or slightly eccentric to wear running leggings. We actually have a divide in the office between guys who go out in leggings all the time and people who think it's a badge of honour to be wearing short shorts. That's less of a technical decision and more of an aesthetic decision.

My own tech-obsessed days ended suddenly on a glorious spring morning in the Lake District when I had one of those eureka moments. I crested a fell, sniffed the unpolluted air, enjoyed the sensation of soft earth under my feet and realised that the gadgets and gear were getting in the way of my running. My enjoyment of it, certainly.

I'm now largely of the opinion that simple is better. It varies from runner to runner, but the tech-related gains are mostly marginal. Mind you, I do still love a pair of posh running socks. Bridgedale lightweight merino ankle-length trail sock for me. But the choice is almost endless. Long, short, compression, expensive, cheap, calf guards …

Compression calf-guarding socks are one of the few running gadgets I do believe in, actually. Maybe it's a placebo effect. I used to have mild Achilles and calf issues, and it could have been just the first few years of running, you have more injuries. But if I'm doing a marathon, I would wear calf guards.

Socks are interesting. The big player in socks over the last few years has been Stance, who've turned the humble sock into a work of art. They've even got a store in Covent Garden. They've made socks cool and they do actually perform well too. But, as a rule, you could probably survive with fairly simple socks, though you need actual running socks from a blister perspective. And blisters are potentially race-ending. So it's quite high stakes with socks.

Also, recently the Injinji running socks, toe socks and ones that just separate the big toe from all other toes. Big in Japan. I quite like those, because I think sometimes blisters can be caused by your toes rubbing together. They mitigate against that.

While we're discussing the feet, the obvious next stop is shoes. And you can't talk about shoes without starting with Nike's controversial Vaporfly. The one Eliud Kipchoge wore to break two hours for the marathon, the one Brigid Kosgei wore the same weekend to shatter Paula Radcliffe's long-standing world record, the one so many runners wore (myself included) in Amsterdam the following week. The one that's doubled Nike's share price.

I mean, that's the biggest change in shoe conversation in our life-times. Even non-runners are now aware of these shoes

It's interesting, isn't it, because the conversation 10 years ago was around barefoot running. Where's that all gone?

It's a shame that barefoot running gets such a bad press now, because the principle of barefoot running – the efficient stride, mid-foot landing – I think that's largely logical.

People got a bit evangelical, myself included actually, about minimalist running. I thought unless you were landing on your forefoot, unless you're running in minimalist shoes, then you're probably running wrong. And the flip side, if you're doing that then you're definitely running right. But in fact, there is a way of running, while landing on your forefoot, that's really unskilled actually and will lead to the same amount of injury – it would just be a different injury.

There's definitely something such as a skilled heel strike. It's actually the way that Mo Farah runs really, a kind of heel touch – it's just heel first. And probably the bigger things to think about are cadence, posture, rhythm, strength ...

I think there is still a place for minimalist shoes. But then we saw Hoka and their Maximalist shoes. When they came in, I kind of thought of them as the monster truck of shoes. I thought they were a bit of a joke actually and then there are people winning races in Hokas.

So, the Vaporfly feel like they are kind of maximalists. But they're also light, very inflexible. Then we talk in the office, how fair is it to put a carbon fibre plate in a shoe? Say you were to finish fourth for the world champ and you were six seconds out from the medals and the three people ahead of you were all wearing Vaporfly and you weren't. Is that fair competition, or is it more like Formula 1, where you have a better car and therefore you win?

I have a club-mate who bought two pairs of Vaporflys. He went to try them out, went for a little run up and down the street. He said, 'I could tell that they were going to give me an advantage and I didn't feel right so I put them online and I sold them again.'

I can guarantee he's in the minority. The Barnes Runners WhatsApp group has become a showcase for new shoes. PBs are being broken in massive, space-age, pink footwear.

At least the humble running top is still relatively simple – and perhaps getting even simpler.

> We have all accepted now that you need a fast-wicking tee shirt. They call them 'technicals'. And something that doesn't completely weigh you down with sweat is useful. But there's a growing trend back to cotton. Several people now say running in cotton tee shirts is great because you can feel the effort you're putting in. It becomes tapestry for your own effort. But from a practical perspective, a wicking tee shirt's a must, especially for a long race like a marathon.
>
> I think we all run best in a vest. Some people feel getting a vest is a big statement, like 'I'm a proper runner.' But when you're racing, get a vest on – you actually feel faster in a vest.

As it happens, I feel faster in a long-sleeved shirt. Although I'm pretty sure that's just me. I have a dark blue shirt which I wore the first time I broke three hours for the marathon, for my first 100-mile race, when I completed the 153-mile Spartathlon – it's now become my go-to top for any important race. I'd be heartbroken if I lost it.

As I would my trusty Garmin.

> Watches have become so complicated now. I was testing one recently, it costs over £500, but it can tell you literally everything. It can almost predict the future. It can tell me how fast I'll run my next marathon.
>
> Each to their own. Everyone's got a different budget and different ambitions. There are certain things you should look for: something that has GPS and tells you your minutes per mile, if you want that. But do some of your runs without a watch, tuning in to how you feel,

doing it on effort rather than data from your wrist. It's a really good skill and actually can be less stressful for runners.

People were good at running before the advent of smart watches. They still found a way to run evenly, so it's very, very do-able without. I don't feel like you'd have to spend 400 quid to do this at all. Get a little Casio!

It's freezing outside on the day we speak and I have a seven-mile run home from the *Runner's World* offices. I'm tempted to ask to borrow some running gloves because my fingers do get freezing, but as Rick reminds me, dress for the second mile:

Gloves and hat are useful in certain scenarios, like if you were far away from any help, out on the trail, off-road, when it's very, very cold. There's nothing wrong with packing these things at all, but I think often you can start with a hat and gloves and within minutes you regret it, because you're like, 'Actually, I'm warming up incredibly quickly.'

A buff is more useful than most other things because it's so versatile. You can wear a buff as a snood or a hat. You can wear it around your wrist if you want to wipe sweat from your forehead. A buff is perhaps a better thing to buy than a hat.

The same principle with rucksacks with bladders. A lot of these things are about feeling secure. When you go off, you've got a big CamelBak on and you're like, 'I'm obviously not going to run out of water.' For most training runs, that's a little bit OTT. There are other solutions such as hand-held bottles, or a running hydration belt. Those things are more appropriate for urban running. And a huge backpack slows you down as well.

As for compression sleeves, Mo wears them, Eliud wears them, but for the life of me I do not understand what they are offering. My editor upstairs, Andy Dixon, he likes them. But partly for warmth. It can be freezing in a start pen for the early spring marathons so you can quite easily roll them down or take them off.

But when I tried them, they started falling down my arms, so maybe it's a few trips to the gym that's required. But honestly, from what I know about locomotion and how to run, I can't see how warming up forearms and biceps is helping.

But nutrition is the area in which we receive the most snake oil-type products. This boosts memory, that kind of claim. We usually don't publish if we don't believe in a product. We're not in the business of just slagging things off.

Before I leave, I find myself wondering about the future of gadgets. I've heard that running in a virtual world, on treadmills, is becoming big news. There could even be a Running World Championships, where the pros come and race each other virtually. Especially if there was money on the table.

Also, similar to the Kipchoge Challenge, where there was that green laser light on the ground, pacing him from a Tesla he was following, soon there could be glasses which project speed, distance and time out in front of you.

But what sort of gadgets would runners like that aren't available currently?

We actually put that exact question out to our readers. What gadgets would you want to see exist? Readers suggested a GPS watch that takes into account distance, gradient, wind speed and gives you a standardised pace. Trainers with self-adapting grips for a multi-terrain run. And my favourite, a tee shirt that shows you how far you're going and how far you've been. So, you know when you're in a park and someone overtakes you and you're a bit like, I'm 17 miles into my long run? Your tee shirt would say, 'Well, actually, this guy's done 17 miles and he's trying to do 22 today.'

But the important thing to remember is, running can be so simple. When you start running, all you need to have is a pair of trainers that feel comfortable. Don't spends loads of money. Get out there and run – and find out what we've all been harping on about!

Wise words. And Rick's parting advice, I think, is the key to all this.

Keep it simple. And then if you feel like it, invest more in your hobby. Definitely that order. Get excited about running, the actual feeling of running.

WHAT TO REMEMBER

- Running first, tech a distant second;
- The only really important bit of kit is a pair of running shoes that work well for you;
- A GPS watch which measures speed and distance can help take your training to the next level;
- Relax, the right equipment will find you when you need it;
- A nice, posh, comfy, new pair of running socks never fails to make you happy.

NUTRITION AND HYDRATION

Tip: A banana makes for an excellent mid-run boost because it's high in carbohydrates, antioxidants and anti-inflammatories. It's also easy to digest for a fast energy boost.

I once ran a marathon in Italy, but ruined it before I started through chronic overindulgence at the hotel breakfast buffet. It was all just too big, too tempting …

Normally, a hotel near the start of a big city marathon will cheerfully lay on a skeleton breakfast of toast and porridge extra-early so the runners can carb up to their hearts' content. Trouble is, this particular hotel, small and friendly and with an almost perfect score on Tripadvisor, went the extra mile and laid out the full monty from 5 a.m. onwards.

Now I don't know about you, but I have real trouble with moderation when faced with a breakfast buffet. Especially one featuring limitless quantities of all my favourite foods. This gluttony is only exacerbated on marathon morning when I can't help feeling I'm about to burn off everything I eat anyway. So essentially, it's guilt-free.

Nine courses later, with *nine full plates* of delicious food sloshing around inside me, I'm wondering why I'm feeling curiously lethargic as I stand on the start line. And then I start running – and realise.

In the pre-race blurb, they claim that during the Rome Marathon, 'you will feel in your heart each of the 42.195 km that you will run.' Well, for me, they were *almost* right. Except it wasn't in my heart that I felt every footstep, but a little lower down – in my stomach. Running the Eternal City marathon as bloated as an ancient Roman after a lavish banquet, it's not ideal.

I've since tried to eat as sensibly as possible before any long race like a marathon but old habits die hard. Which is why I'm privileged to know Anita Bean. Her books, *The Runner's Cookbook* and *The Vegetarian Athlete's Cookbook*, are the most battered in our kitchen. (Battered, as in well-used, that is, not battered as in deep-fried.) She has several simple rules when it comes to planning your running diet:

First, there's your main fuel, so that's your carbohydrate. That's what provides your muscles with energy, to allow you to run. For most runners that should form about one third of your plate. But having said that, it will really depend on the length and the intensity of your planned workout so obviously the more intense workout you're doing, if you're doing hills, if you are doing many, many miles, you will need more carbohydrates than somebody who's perhaps just trotting around the block for 10 minutes.

The second thing that you need to remember in your meal is adding in some protein. So, that's the building blocks. That's what's going to repair your muscles after each gruelling run. And the third thing you want to think about, that's your fruit and veg for your 'fighting nutrients', the fibre, the vitamins, minerals, all of these really good things that are going to keep you super healthy, allow you to recover effectively from your runs.

And you also want to include a little bit of the healthy fats. They supply these essential fatty acids that are really important for recovery and also for improving your performance in your runs. So these things are olive oil, oily fish (if you eat that), nuts and seeds, and avocados.

These days at the finish line of any major marathon, you tend to be given a goody bag. In among the banana, coconut water and flapjack there may well be some kind of 'recovery protein'. I was once even offered a protein beer. I refused, then regretted doing so.

Recovering is the critical thing. When you're running, you're breaking down your muscle tissue. What you do afterwards builds strength, aerobic fitness and endurance. So, the easiest way to remember recovery is the three Rs: rehydration, refuelling and repair.

First, putting back in the carbohydrates that you've just burned, but obviously, just the right amounts. Also the protein, and that will help to rebuild those muscle fibres that you've just broken down. These are equally important when following a vegetarian/vegan diet. And finally, we're talking about rehydrating, putting back the fluid that you've sweated out.

All the research at the moment is pointing to the benefits of milk. And that can be dairy or non-dairy milk, because they both supply all of those components as well as various other vitamins and minerals. So, anything based on milk or yoghurt, or vegan types if you prefer that, would be really good. But at the end of the day, a good old banana or a cheese sandwich and some fruit will actually be also really good for improving and promoting the recovery that you need after each run.

Clearly in Rome, when I basically ate the entire buffet spread a few hours before setting off, I was making a rookie error. But, according to Anita, runners frequently do the opposite, which is equally damaging to their race hopes:

> I often see marathon runners inadvertently under-fuelling. It's so easy to underestimate how much energy you're burning, even in training. And what happens if you do that day after day, and week after week, you're not putting the fuel and nutrients back into your body. And what can happen is that you'll notice that your energy levels drop, that you are struggling to recover properly after each run. You will notice that perhaps you're becoming more prone to illnesses, you're picking up more colds and coughs, and minor ailments like that. And maybe also you become more prone to injuries.

I've always found it difficult to find the right eating balance during the taper. As Race Day approaches and running load decreases, I'll frequently find myself either over- or under-eating. Sometimes I'll make myself miserable by carb-starving at the start of race week, followed the gradual, bliss-ful carb-load from Wednesday onwards. I've experimented with vitamins, supplements, oils, gels, you name it. Paula Radcliffe famously drinks half a pint of Guinness on marathon eve. But what should we be doing? Is carb-loading even still a thing? Apparently so.

Yes, you definitely want to increase the amount of carbohydrate you're consuming for the final two to three days before the marathon. Pasta, potatoes, rice, bananas, all of those lovely foods. So you're gradually eating more of those foods, but on the other hand, you're eating a little bit less fat, because you want to keep the calories about the same. Obviously, you don't want to be gaining weight in the last couple of days before the marathon and end up feeling rather heavy and sluggish.

And it doesn't mean having a massive pasta party the night before. The way it's done nowadays is to taper your training for the last two, three weeks before the marathon. So it's a gradual reduction in intensity, and automatically there will be a gradual replenishment in your glycogen.

Glycogen gives our muscles energy, it's our body's natural Duracell AA battery. But the problem with a marathon is that we've only got enough glycogen to last for around two hours, which for recreational runners is a maximum of 18 to 20 miles. And when we run out of glycogen, that's when we hit the dreaded Wall. Which means ideally, we'd refuel on the run. Runners have different tastes. Some can rely on energy gels to give them that all-important mid-race momentum, others feel sick at the thought of them. Many get the nutrients they need from energy drinks, others from bananas and jelly babies.

Mark Kennedy is a runner and coach in Canada who used to live near me in London and now runs an ace website for runners, *www.nonetorun.com*. A US Track and Field certified coach and a former kinesiologist, he gave me his top 10 tips for fuelling marathons.

1. TEST DIFFERENT TYPES OF FUEL

Runners have different tastes. Some people can chug back energy gels like they are shots of water. Others, like me, struggle with the consistency and texture. Some runners can't bear chewing something while running, some don't have an issue with it.

You need to find the type of fuel that works for you from both a taste and texture standpoint. Go to your local running shop or favourite online running store and order a bunch of different gels, chews, jellybeans and sports drinks. Within your order, be sure to get the types of fuel (gels/chews and sports drink) that will be offered in your race. This will save you from carrying your own fuel during the race (which isn't a big deal if you need to) if they agree with you. Try them all on your training runs and see what you like.

2. THE BEST FUEL IS A COMBINATION OF GLUCOSE AND FRUCTOSE

Current research shows that using fuels that contain a combination of glucose and fructose is optimal. Glucose and fructose are carried across the intestinal wall to the bloodstream by two different transporters.

If you're consuming a glucose-only fuel, the amount of energy that enters the bloodstream will be limited. By taking in a mix of glucose and fructose, you take advantage of additional transporters that will move fructose into the bloodstream as well. Most gels and chews these days contain a combination of both. Often, you will see maltodextrin as an ingredient, which is glucose as well. Check the labels to see what you're consuming.

3. THE RULE OF 15

Most marathoners know they need to fuel, but don't know how much.

Enter the Rule of 15.

Fifteen grams of carbohydrate every 15 minutes – or 60 grams of carbs per hour. Every hour.

Of course, some runners will be able to handle this amount of carbohydrate, others will not and may need to start at 30 grams and progress up from there.

Most energy gels provide approximately 25 grams of carbohydrate. And don't forget, you can obtain some of these carbohydrates from a sports drink.

So, to get 60 grams of carbohydrate in an hour, you would need to consume two gels and 75 ml of energy drink.

4. PRACTISE, PRACTISE, PRACTISE

Fuelling for a marathon is not something you should wing, especially if you care at all about your time and having an enjoyable race experience.

- Practise the amount of fuel you take in. Some runners will be able to handle more than others. Start practising at 30 grams (about 1 gel) of carbs per hour and work your way up;
- Practise taking fuel from your belt while actually running;

- Practise your fuelling strategy on five to six long runs and ensure you do so at your goal (or close to your goal) marathon pace. The physical and mental demands of running at your goal pace will provide the best simulation of what you'll encounter on Race Day. Practising your fuelling on an easy 10k run is just not the same;
- Document how much fuel you consumed on each run and how you felt.

5. EXPERIMENT WITH CAFFEINE

Ever wondered why caffeine is often found in many pain medications?

Caffeine has been shown to block the processing of pain signals on the central nervous system. In a marathon, caffeine's effects will help you focus more and block some of the pain associated with the efforts related to running 42.2 kilometres.

Aim to take in 100 to 200 milligrams of caffeine about 30–60 minutes prior to your race. During the race, 25 or 50 milligrams per hour will provide a top-up and give you benefits later in the race when you really need them. For reference, a tall Americano from Starbucks provides about 150 milligrams of caffeine.

6. SQUEEZE YOUR CUP

Drinking from those paper cups at aid stations without stopping and spilling more water on your face than gets into your mouth is difficult. Simple tip here, and it may seem like common sense, but not everyone does it: when you grab a cup of water or sports drink from the aid station, slightly squeeze the top of the cup to make the top opening smaller (like a water bottle). Now drink through the narrow opening. You'll get much more fluid into you and less on your shirt.

7. STUDY THE RACE COURSE

You don't want any surprises on Race Day, so study the race course and know exactly where every aid station is and what type of fuel they'll offer (brand of gels and sports drink).

Organise with a friend or family member to be at a specific spot on the marathon race course (preferably around the 30-km mark when most runners start hitting the Wall) and give them some backup gels and sports drink. You may not need the extra fuel, but it's reassuring to know it will be there, should you accidentally drop some of the fuel you are carrying or just need an extra boost.

8. START FUELLING EARLY

Don't wait until you're starting to feel tired before you fuel. Start fuelling as early as 15 minutes into the race in order to hit the optimal amount of 60 grams of carbohydrate per hour.

9. YOU MIGHT HAVE TO CARRY YOUR OWN FUEL (AND THAT'S OKAY)

If you're not going to rely on the fuel offered on the marathon course, you will need to carry your own. There are lots of different belts and waist packs available to get the job done. They're not expensive, uncomfortable or heavy.

10. HYDRATION NEEDS ARE WEATHER-DEPENDENT

The weather largely dictates how much fluid you should take in during your marathon. Running a marathon in Hawaii, for example, will require much more fluid intake than an early spring marathon in Toronto.

Let thirst be your guide, but a lack of thirst on a cool day does not mean you require any less carbohydrates. Using sports drinks will help you meet both your hydration and carbohydrate needs. Research shows that optimising your hydration and carbohydrate needs can improve your marathon performance from 2–20 per cent, depending on your current level of fitness and running experience. While 2 per cent does not sound like much, it equates to two and a half minutes for a 2:15 runner. Those two and a half minutes are the difference between qualifying for the marathon World Championships and watching them on TV. For a four-hour runner, a 5 per cent improvement sheds 12 minutes from your time, placing you in the 'sub 3:50' club. So, if you really want to run a marathon to your potential and not just 'get by' or 'grind it out', you must make fuelling a priority.

Fuelling, yes, including hydration, obviously. I once had my sweat tested by the experts at Precision Hydration. I found out I sweat A LOT (which I kind of already knew) but don't lose too much salt when I do so. Andy Blow founded the company, having frequently struggled with cramp and other hydration issues during his career as an elite triathlete:

One of the common misconceptions is people thinking: 'If I lose one litre of sweat an hour – which is around average – then I need to replace one litre an hour.' In almost all circumstances, you can get away with drinking considerably less than you're sweating out. You just need to drink enough to keep performance levels up. When you finish a marathon, you should actually be a little dehydrated. The body's designed to work like that.

But if you become severely dehydrated, that's when problems occur. The fundamental problem is that you reduce your blood volume because your sweat comes from your blood. And when you're also trying to exercise, you're trying to pump as much blood as you can to the muscles and to the skin for cooling. So, if you become dehydrated, it makes the exercise harder, your heart rate goes up and your perception of effort increases dramatically. That will invariably cause your performance to slow down.

However, the bigger problem is over hydration. If you drink a larger amount of fluid than you're getting rid of, then you actually start to dilute the salt levels in your body and in your blood specifically. That's called hyponatraemia and it can cause you to become very ill. What the body does is shifts fluid from the bloodstream into your cells to store it there to stop the salt levels getting too low in the blood. But those cells expand, and if your brain cells expand, your brain crushes itself against the inside of your skull and you can get neurological damage. Headaches, seizures, coma and, very occasionally, even death.

The ideal is to find the sweet spot in the middle. It's actually not especially difficult, the same sort of thing as learning your pacing. So, listen to your body and you'll get to the stage where how much fluid to take on board becomes intuitive.

WHAT TO REMEMBER

- Experiment with different gels and sports drinks to see which (if any) work for you;
- Stay hydrated, but beware: over-hydration is more dangerous;
- In the days before the marathon, increase the amount of carbs in your diet – not the overall calories;
- Your glycogen (muscle energy) stores only last around two hours; after that, you'll need to replenish them;
- Post-race, try to get some protein inside you as soon as possible to repair damaged muscle fibres.

WOMEN'S RUNNING

'If you want to be the best runner you can be, start now.'
Priscilla Welch, British Olympic marathon runner

I first meet Esther Newman, the editor of *Women's Running* magazine, at the pasta party on the eve of the Loch Ness Marathon. We spend 10 minutes comparing notes on how much our respective five-year-olds enjoy junior parkrun. We then spend the next hour bemoaning the sexism that still exists, scarcely believably, in the sport we both love.

It's legacy sexism mainly. This is the way it's always been. Cross country is the worst culprit, with inequality in race distance plain weird:

Senior women 8k, senior men 15k
Under-20 women 6k, Under-20 men 8k
Under-17 women 5k, Under-17 men 6k
Under-15 girls 4k, Under-15 boys 4.5k

I'm delighted to discover Esther feels even more strongly than I do and instigates a protest at the following January's National Championships.

That final one is the kicker – just half a kilometre, which amounts to a couple of minutes at most, and makes girls think that they cannot achieve the same distances – and cannot be judged by the same standards – as boys from a very young age. This tiny distance discrepancy leads to the situation where exceptional, fast adult women athletes don't believe they should – or could – run that 15k distance but of course they wouldn't bat an eye at running a marathon, three times the distance, alongside men.

It's absolutely ludicrous. One of the main things that astounds me is that girls are being taught that for some reason they should be running a shorter distance than boys. You can't quite make five kilometres, so why don't you run four? That's what it's saying.

One of the defences has been that women take longer to run in general than the men, so that the timings would have to be increased and therefore it would cost more money to hold the championships. It's not an answer, is it? Not in the era of Jasmin Paris, or frankly, why in the era of being able to vote, would you say to women, 'You can't run the same distance as men'? It's absolutely ridiculous.

Jasmin Paris is the fell runner who became the first woman to win the 268-mile Montane Spine Race along the Pennine Way – and inadvertently catapulted her sport into the mainstream. The race took her a shade over 83 hours, which broke the overall record, men's and women's, by 12 hours. All while pausing to express breastmilk at aid stations.

As a keen fell runner myself, I've chatted to her several times, before and since. I catch up with Jasmin again when we're sat next to each other at the *Sunday Times* Sportswoman of the Year Awards in central London, where she is presented with the Helen Rollason Award for Inspiration.

It's a privilege to have so many people telling me they've been inspired, and I'm very grateful for that. I feel like this is an opportunity to show what I believe about gender equality – through action.

Jasmin took her sport – and message – mainstream in the wake of those 83 gruelling hours. As well as training twice a day most days, she's a mum, a vet and studying for a PhD. How she makes the time, I have no idea.

I sort of feel I'm just having fun and I happen to be good at this. I think what I do in science is more serious and more important. But fell running is a very open community, very friendly. Even racing, championship racing, the very elite runners will be racing with the very slowest runners and there's no distinction. When you're lined up for your tea and cake at the end, there's absolutely no elitism in this sport. It's lovely. It's so welcoming to anyone, and I think that goes hand in hand with the ethos of being outdoors in the mountains.

Interesting to note, over longer distances, the physical differences between men and women stop being an issue:

It's less about strength and more about stamina. I'm lucky to have this platform, to get a message out to other women. The story about taking part in sport, about breastfeeding, those kinds of issues, I truly believe in them. I just try to lead by example. It's nice that people seem interested.

People are more than interested. Interested enough to offer book and film deals, which are politely declined. But while Jasmin inspires thousands with her remarkable talent, achievements and modesty, Esther Newman's passion is to promote inclusivity and equality within running. It's why she took the job at *Women's Running*:

> Women need the space to be able to discuss their running separately from men because there are different needs and there's different stuff to be talked about. When I first started at the magazine, I remember speaking to a non-runner, who said to me, 'Is there enough to talk about to do a monthly magazine about running?' There is too much. From a gear point of view, but also from a political perspective as well as just the distances, the training, everything. We can talk about pregnancy and big boobs and hormones and safety issues – if that's on another running magazine, it puts off about 50 per cent of their readership. On our magazine, I'd hope that it would put off a very small percentage.
>
> On the current front cover are Connie and Stacy. They're sisters and they've just run a half-marathon. One of our big things is that we feature real women on the cover that lead into real interviews on the inside. We never use a model on the cover. Never. We always use women who have run amazing distances or achieved great things through their running and then we talk to them inside. I think it's ridiculous that you wouldn't want to hear more about these people. And Connie and Stacy, it's a lovely story. We've been training them to run to a half-marathon distance comfortably. I mean, why would you put them on the cover and then not speak to them inside, or why would you have them inside and not have them on the cover?

The most obvious dilemma faced by women runners (and never by men!) is about running during pregnancy. And just after:

Yeah, we've just done a feature on that actually, because obviously, we get a lot of women writing in who are concerned, especially high-impact exercise like running. But you know your own body. If you've always run, then carry on whilst pregnant within reason. I go to a boot camp, where there's a woman who's pregnant with twins. And so she's up at 6.20 a.m. with the rest of us doing burpees, but she does adapt. And you can be sensible. Sometimes it's just not very comfortable to run with a great big bump in front of you.

There have been some new guidelines about running post-pregnancy. They used to say, 'Start running six weeks after giving birth.' And that was the only information you were given. Now they're suggesting, actually it's much longer and you need to build up to it gradually. It can be a little bit depressing if you're really looking forward to getting out there again because you haven't been able to do it for quite a while, especially in the latter stages of pregnancy. But just be super careful about reintroducing exercise. Low-impact, strength exercise to begin with, and then work your way up to walking and running as you would normally if you were just starting running, in the knowledge that you will increase and get better, much, much quicker than you would have done if you'd never run before.

And I can't emphasise the pelvic floor exercises enough.

My friend and colleague Rachel Horne, Virgin Radio news supremo and formerly of the BBC News Channel and Newsround, never thought she could train for a marathon, having had three difficult births in five years. On air and off, Rachel frequently advocates the importance of pelvic floor exercises. Flick through any issue of *Women's Running* and you realise she is far from alone in this:

> It's really, really boring, but pelvic floor exercises are an absolute must. I think something that really helps is to do them while you're pregnant. But that doesn't mean that everything's all over and done with if you're not.
>
> The exercises in themselves, I think, have changed a lot in the last five years. The general zip and tuck has changed to something much more gradual and controlled. If you go to Pilates, which I strongly recommend, it includes all of the pelvic floor exercises.

I heard about a couple who had the idea of putting little round stickers wherever they might be standing still for any length of time in the house, in front of the sink, at the end of the shower, above the telly. Whenever they spotted the stickers, they would involuntarily do the pelvic floor tuck.

Rachel thought she was the last person to be able to run a marathon. But she successfully completed London, even with a minor hip injury. But it was midway through training for the marathon when she realised she was winning:

> I was doing these sessions with a physio called Emma James and one day I did a three-mile run and I was dry for the first time. The feeling of elation over that, you cannot imagine.

The NHS have a useful app to help with pelvic floor exercises. And on their website there's the helpful guidance – if you've got a big race coming up – that you can delay your period if you're taking the contraceptive pill. You just keep taking it.

Which is one of the other big issues that bypasses male runners: running around periods.

There's a groundbreaking new app called Wild AI, helping women train, fuel and recover based on the menstrual cycle. The cycle is split into five stages and the training diary adjusted accordingly. It's the brainchild of trail runner and ice swimmer Hélène Guillaume. She's so busy, she attaches her diary to the bottom of emails so you can find a rare time slot when she's available and schedule yourself in for a chat.

When you are a woman, we have advantages having a menstrual cycle, which means that sometimes a body is really able to push and do a lot of high-intensity workouts. But if you are not training with the cycle, you basically go against the natural needs of the body in terms of nutrition, training and recovery. If you are going with it, you can not only reduce the symptoms, but you also increase your performance. To give you some examples, in the first two phases, when you have periods and then just after, that's a good thing for cardiovascular workouts and strength.

Then ovulation time would be your body saying, 'Well, you need to be open up to external events,' for instance, if you were procreating. So, basically, the immune system is lowering and the body opens up as well to get pregnant every single month. So, ACL injury is a very common injury correlated to ovulation time. Also, at ovulation time, when the immune system lowers, it is best to keep cardiovascular work at low intensity. And it becomes also harder to recover, usually, from higher-end cardiovascular strain.

And then we enter phase four, which is just after ovulation before you have any symptoms. The immune response has changed and you have more anti-inflammatory increase of oestrogen, progesterone. This is a great phase for a longer super workout and a great time to go to the gym.

And the last phase, which is not very positive for women who are experiencing premenstrual symptoms. So, it's actually a really nice time to de-load, from a training perspective. You should focus more on things like technique, movement, efficiency. Here, the immune system is still anti-inflammatory, but oestrogen and progesterone begin to drop, so this alters balance, cognition and reaction, and increases the central nervous system fatigue.

Jo Pavey is a British athletics legend. She competed in five consecutive Olympic Games in the 5,000 and 10,000m: starting in Sydney in 2000, then a fantastic fifth place in Athens, a PB in Beijing, another at her home Games in London 2012. When she sensationally qualified for Rio in 2016, she was famously wearing a vest that was older than many of her competitors.

In 2014, in Zurich, aged 40, Jo became the oldest-ever European champion, storming to gold in the 10,000m. She's also won medals at World Championships and Commonwealth Games. And making her achievements and longevity even more remarkable, she's been a mum since 2009. She won that gold in Zurich 10 months after giving birth to her second child, Emily:

I love running, I love everything about it. I love the feeling of freedom, getting out into the countryside, running in beautiful places. And then I'm trying to hit targets and training, I like the challenge of that, and the challenge of the races ... it's exciting. And having goals gives you some focus.

I think anyone who wants to take up running can set themselves a goal. It doesn't have to be too serious, just enjoy your running and have something to aim for.

Running also gives me a chance to gather my thoughts and think about what I'm going to do later in the day, get myself organised. Or let my mind wander. Sometimes I imagine songs in my head. Running easily refreshes my mind really. It's quite a de-stresser, being out there and running – and when I get back in, I end up feeling better and fresher.

And now that I'm a mum, it's important to show my kids that it's good to be healthy. I don't think I'm ever going to retire literally from running – I'm always going to run because I love it. I love the way it makes you feel good about yourself, boosts your self-esteem and it's fun to feel fit. I'll definitely keep doing it until I'm well into old age.

Not that Jo's had it easy. She had to fight discrimination along the way. Along with several high-profile American runners, she claimed Nike discriminated against pregnant athletes by cutting off payments. She was dropped by Nike as a sponsored athlete shortly after becoming European champion. The company also apparently froze her sponsorship after she became pregnant with each of her children.

It is important for companies to look at messages they are sending out. They are promoting women, saying, 'Come on, dream your dreams, you can achieve things.' But then, when they are under circumstances like becoming a mum, they are signifying that could end their goals and that is definitely the wrong message.

It's not just running. In sport in general, women haven't had their voices heard for far too long. But sport is changing from the top down. Wimbledon now has equal prize money and one day soon, I hope to see the women's final on the Sunday afternoon – why not alternate years with the men's? The football landscape was changed forever by the 2019 World Cup in France when over a billion people watched Megan Rapinoe and the USA team storm to victory.

Athletics has often lagged behind – it was 1984 before women were allowed to run an Olympic marathon – but people like Jasmin, Jo and Esther, and charities such as Women in Sport and 261 Fearless are now leading the change. It's inspirational to watch.

WHAT TO REMEMBER

- Take medical advice and listen to your body when considering running during pregnancy;
- Men's physiological advantage decreases with distance, so much so that many of the longer overall trail running records are held by women;
- Consider training differently at different stages of the menstrual cycle.

RESTORATIVE RUNNING

'There is something magical about running; after a certain distance, it transcends the body. Then a bit further, it transcends the mind. A bit further yet, and what you have before you, laid bare, is the soul.'
Kristin Armstrong, 'See Vous Play', *Runner's World* **magazine**

The question I'm most often asked: *why do you run?* Here's my answer: I run for fitness. I run for escape. For therapy. Discovery. Self-discovery. I run for the simple, childlike joy of running when you could be walking. Running has given me some of the best friends I could ever hope to make. It's taken me to some weird and wonderful places. It's an ever-unfolding adventure. And most of all, I'll say it again and I'll say it forever, you NEVER regret a run.

And that usually does it. An honest, fulsome answer. Generally, people don't probe any further.

But sometimes they do persist. Why did you start? Are you running towards or away from something? And I don't usually answer those questions, because the answer is painful. I won't indulge myself by getting into details, but generally I'm running away. It's why I used to abhor being overtaken. Over the years, running helped calm the demons and these days, if you edge ahead of me in Richmond Park, I may even be happy to let you go.

Ben Smith once ran 401 marathons in 401 days for anti-bullying charities. Along with his husband, Kyle, he now runs the 401 Foundation, supporting local community projects. None of this would have happened without the marathons:

Finding running was more of a shock to me than anybody. Four years ago, I didn't even run. I got into it, I suppose, by accident. It was a friend of mine that spoke up. He was sick and tired of me moaning and groaning about the fact that I should get fit and healthy, because I'd suffered from what they call a TIA, a Transient Ischaemic Attack (a sort of temporary stroke), about a year before. That made me sit up and realise that my life had to change, but I didn't know how that was going to happen. I was 16½ stone (105 kg) and a 30-a-day smoker. My confidence and self-esteem were at rock bottom. It doesn't happen overnight. I had to figure out what made me happy.

A friend introduced me to my local running club. I remember turning up on the first day and thinking, 'I don't belong here. How can this fat guy run?' I'd never even liked running. I'd never liked sports. This just was not me. But something in my head just ... it pushed me to do it, I tell you: that first night, I ran. Well, I'd like to say I ran, but I walked most of it. I did three miles and it was a sense of pride inside myself. It was a warm feeling that I'd actually achieved something that I'd never done before. I really liked that feeling.

Obviously, I wanted more of that, so I kept on going. I kept going every week, every week, and I grew to love running. It was tough to begin with, don't get me wrong. And there were days where I was just like, 'Oh, no, I don't want to do this anymore.' But I kept at it and my confidence grew. My self-esteem grew. I grew as a person. I grew into liking myself again. Especially from a mental health point of view, it seemed to be my opportunity to escape and to rid myself of all the stress that I had in my life. It's a cliché but it was a way to find myself again, find who I really was.

I was running home from work one day when I bumped into – literally – a young man running towards a better version of himself. It was on Hammersmith Bridge in West London. I was flat out, trying to break my work-to-home record. Ryan (not his real name) was coming fast the other way. We flew towards one of the large, green buttresses from opposite directions. Unable to see each other, we each went around and – bang! The resulting clash of heads knocked us both to the ground.

For one terrifying moment, I thought he was going to fight me. His eyes flashed with anger, his hands formed briefly into fists. But Ryan's rush of rage receded almost as quickly. We were soon sitting down together to recover from the collision and he ended up recounting his running story. He let me record it on my phone, as long as I didn't use his real name. Which, it only occurred to me later, he never told me anyway.

I was in lots of fights. Lots of other trouble. The way I was heading, I was maybe heading inside. I was angry all the time, looking for reasons to kick off and I didn't care about myself, or anything. Then my mate's uncle, he said I should try running with him. I just went in my normal clothes, my mate's uncle said that was fine. I'm glad I said yes. Couple of days later, I went for a run by myself. Not long, just 10 minutes or something, but when I got back I realised I was pleased with myself and maybe that was the first time, properly. It's like, when you've done something good, and feeling good not horrible, and after that you chase after the good feeling again. It made a big difference for me.

I'm running now three times a week. Four, maybe. One week, I ran every day. And I'm much calmer, like my attitude has improved. It's like I respect myself, and if I feel respected, then I'm okay. Also, it's shown me I can push myself and improve. Get faster and go further. And now, I rarely ever even think about doing the same things that I was doing back then. It's like I'm running now and I'm going the right way.

I thought of Ryan when I first watched the brilliant documentary film, *Skid Row Marathon*. It's the inspiring true story of an unlikely group of homeless runners from LA's Skid Row. Recovering addicts, paroled convicts, a single mum, a softly spoken man who spent three decades in prison for murder. And they all train for marathons with a man who'd previously sentenced some of them to prison, Superior Court Judge Craig Mitchell, founder of the Skid Row Running Club.

With his California suntan, square jaw and bulging biceps, Judge Mitchell looks every inch the movie star. So much so that when you're watching the film, you have to keep reminding yourself that this is real life. Actually, as real as it gets.

Very much so. I mean, I'm not a movie star, I'm just a judge that sits in the courthouse and hears cases that normally carry life sentences. That's my real world. And my other real world obviously is that I participate in this running programme. About eight blocks away from the courthouse is Skid Row and that's where in excess of 8,000 homeless individuals make their home.

It started out very humbly. I don't know, people I think are innately pretty good reads of other people. They understand if you're down there for some ego trip or if there's some ulterior motive and there wasn't on my part and it was just simply I wanted to share the running experience with other people. I knew what it did for me on a daily basis and I think they figured me out pretty quickly that I was a reasonable guy to spend an hour or two running with.

We're chatting as Judge Mitchell sits in his chambers, one Thursday morning. He's somehow reached out to people who in many cases are on the very cliff edge of society. Why does he think running helps so many different people?

Well, if you read the studies, clearly there's the physiological benefits of running. A few years back, I read an article in *Runner's World* that essentially talked about what goes on in the brain when you run and the release of the dopamine and all those good things. And what really struck me about that article was that there are recovery programmes here in the United States that if you do not agree to run, they will not accept you into the programme because the link between running on a regular basis and being able to maintain your sobriety is really, really clear.

So, there's that aspect of it. Equally important for our participants, our club members, is the sense of community that one enjoys. We run Mondays, Thursdays and Saturdays so you know that three days a week for several hours you're going to be around people that care about you, that are willing to listen to what you have to say to them. We celebrate birthdays together. Somebody gets a job, someone returns after relapsing on drugs or alcohol. I mean, all that is part of our life in the running community and it's very, very important.

All of the runners testify about how running has given them a newfound discipline and determination to overcome their troubled pasts. Single mother Rebecca's heroin and alcohol dependency led to her sleeping rough with her young son. She's now looking for work as a surgical technician. Ben had a promising heavy-metal career ahead of him – 'working with a monster producer, meeting all my heroes, everything I've ever wanted – and I'm not happy. I totalled three cars on the way to the liquor store, then got out of jail and drank as much as I could, just hoping to die.' The running club gives him the confidence to study at the San Francisco Conservatory of Music.

David, who lived on the streets for 10 years, is trying to become an artist. And Rafael now spends his days warning children against following a life of crime. He's a gentle soul, a dignified man. Hard to reconcile the fact that he served 28 years in prison for murder.

And of course the Skid Row Running Club is bigger than it is in the film. There are many others who've come to rely on it to get their lives back on track.

Miguel, for example:

I played a little bit of recreational soccer. Other than that, there was no running at all. I needed something strict, like doing something on a consistent basis, and something I never had before. I needed a group of people with a positive mindset to take away the negativity of my life earlier on – it was all negativity. That's why I joined. I wouldn't do it without the high fives or just people showing up. That means a lot. It helps my self-esteem and the way I look at things. And I'm setting goals, something I've never cared for before. It's endless. I chose a sport that is endless, because you can always get better.

And Derek:

April 8th, 2015 – I left Memphis to come out here to recover from alcoholism. I always knew that once you get rid of one habit, you have to replace it with a new habit. I lost my job one time and wasn't doing good in school and those were triggers. You feel it and you don't want to feel it. You want to numb this failure that you put yourself through and you know how to do it, because you've done it for 40 years. I couldn't go back because of running. I couldn't disappoint them, I couldn't disappoint myself. So, the running club kept me sober and as I do it, things start coming back together for me – the school and the job – I kept going forward. If I didn't have the running club, me and you wouldn't be talking now. I'd be back in my addiction and I'd be back in Memphis.

So, does Judge Mitchell believe running marathons has a more powerful effect when life may have taken a bit of a left turn?

It does. You don't hit rock bottom because of your addiction without alienating a lot of people. A lot of the folks down on Skid Row who begin to involve themselves in our programme are pretty lonely people. Their families are tired of them. Their kids don't want anything to do with them if they have children. And so to be able to connect with other people who are non-judgemental is something that they go, 'Oh my goodness, I really didn't think that I could regain this part of my life.' And running does that.

But what about the man who started this whole thing; how did Judge Mitchell become a 'marathoner'?

I was a prosecutor at the time, a new prosecutor, and there is a law enforcement run here in California called Baker to Vegas and there are about 200 teams. Some of them are fielded from law enforcement in Great Britain. And my boss in the Prosecutor's Office asked if I would run on the Prosecutor's team. And since I didn't really want to torpedo my early career as a prosecutor by saying no to my boss, I said yes. And I was 40 years old at the time and much to my surprise, I really took to it.

The Skid Row Running Club has now been alive and well for eight years. And so we have a track record. The movies left off with us hoping to go to Jerusalem. Well, we went to Jerusalem with 44 of our runners. We subsequently went to Vietnam. We've been to Berlin. We just got back from the Galápagos Islands. So the club is doing really well, the numbers are much greater than those represented in the movie.

And the more the movie has gotten out, the donations have come and it makes us able to buy new shoes for everybody, to go on trips. We also, you mentioned that the parkrun did a programme in one of the prisons in England, well, we go up to San Quentin, we go down Donovan State Prison. A lot of our participants have spent time in prison and for them to be able to go back and nurture a running community in a prison is something that they get a big kick out of. And a lot of the inmates in prison write to me regularly, share their running accomplishments. So the things that have happened as a result of the running club are things I would have never predicted eight years ago when I went down and corralled two or three runners to join me on an afternoon run.

The Skid Row Running Club was founded in 2012 'to provide a running program for the Skid Row Community of Los Angeles and to involve the larger community in supporting its members in overcoming alcohol/drug abuse and achieving positive life goals'. It focuses on five key area as it seeks to empower its members:

1. Developing a dedicated running programme to keep its participants focused on their health and well-being.
2. Providing mentor and mentee relationships.
3. Scheduling charity, fundraising and volunteer events to enable the larger Los Angeles community to help.
4. Participating in local, national and international running events to provide participants with opportunities for personal growth by being exposed to new locales, cultures and people.
5. To develop a commitment to give back to others.

In among all of that, I'm sure Judge Mitchell sees enough stories for a sequel. How about a *Skid Row Marathon 2*?

With every new member, there's an engaging story. That's the thing that I think the movie does such a great job in really making people understand about people who are marginalised, people who are easily dismissed with labels – alcoholics, convicts, etc. If you move past those labels, that one-dimensional view, you're going to find a human being that possesses as much depth and complexity as anybody else. Whatever your background. And that's what's great about the three days that we run together. Yes, they call me 'Judge' because it's just easier than remembering my name, but there's no distinction between any of us.

And that's also the wonderful thing about the start line of any marathon. Everyone lines up next to each other, whatever walk of life they've come from. The wildly wealthy banker standing beside the recovering addict. The butcher beside the baker, beside the candlestick maker. Everyone feeling the same nerves. Everyone focused on the same 26.2-mile goal. Everyone with the same label: marathon runner.

WHAT TO REMEMBER

- Marathons give you discipline and determination which will help in all walks of life;
- Running has been proven to greatly reduce stress and improve mental health;
- You never, never, never regret a run!

RACE DAY

'Courage to start, strength to endure, resolve to finish.'
Unknown

I've made almost every conceivable mistake on Race Day. I can be a little slapdash.

After months of training, I've turned up on the marathon start line hungover, hungry, dehydrated or overtired. I've overdone my running during marathon week and felt utterly drained before the race even begins.

I've frequently forgotten something important. My race number on numerous occasions. The right clothing. I've been late and almost missed the start. I've been too early and frozen solid by the time I started running. I once trained hard for the London Marathon, early January to late April, only to discover that I had, in fact, clean forgotten to enter. And I found myself on the start line of my first ultra-marathon, a 100k race across the Chiltern Hills, without any running shoes. I'd left both pairs by the front door as I set off from the house that morning and had to run for over 11 hours cross country in what were basically brogues.

Race Day is difficult enough, even when you get the logistics spot on. Any marathon is an experience that will assail the senses and there'll *always* be something you hadn't considered, something nobody had warned you about.

Starting with the expo. Expos can seem a little manic, but definitely kind of cool. If in doubt, just ask a volunteer to point you to the right place to pick up your race number, then try not to spend too much money on all that lovely running merch on offer. At expos, I've been known to book running holidays, subscribe to running magazines and buy so much gear that carrying it home wears me out more than the marathon that follows. Oh, and don't forget the safety pins!

Over the years, I've found that the less I leave to chance, the better my Race Day experience. In the days beforehand, it's good advice to consider how to get to the start. And indeed, how to get home again. I've learned (the hard way) that I should lay out my race kit the night before and pin my number to my vest or running shirt. And make sure my name is on there too. It's amazing how personalised cheers galvanise aching legs.

Don't worry unduly if you can't sleep the night before your marathon. I've covered six Olympic Games and hardly any athlete gets a good night's sleep on the eve of their event. It's all fine. It takes sleep 36 hours to benefit the body, so do try to get your eight hours the night before the night before.

On race morning, there will invariably be many more people surrounding you than in any previous race. The New York Marathon has 50,000 finishers, London, Paris, Chicago 40,000. The starting area resembles a small town. This can be intimidating. But while you may be in the same race as thousands of others, in the end the contest is between you and the distance. Don't be put off by what anyone else is doing; they're almost certainly as nervous as you are.

Around the start area, there will be people launching into lavish stretches and embarking on strident warm-up runs, kicking their bum with their heels and/or lifting their knees above their waist. I still feel under pressure when I see them. Should I be doing similar? What do they know that I don't? I've run loads of these races, but maybe it would all be much easier if I did proper warm-ups like that.

The thing is, while I'm sure they're doing the right things for their race, it always strikes me that I'm going to need every ounce of energy to propel me 26.2 miles to the finish line. I can't be doing with expending useless energy before I even start. So I leave them to it.

Drop bags can also be complicated. You're usually allowed a bag to leave at the start/finish area, or which will be driven to the finish for you if it's a point-to-point race. I've frequently brought too little, often too much. Some essentials: Vaseline or plasters to prevent bleeding nipples, a bin liner for a cold, wet morning, a full water bottle to sip, a change of clothes for the finish. Some runners like a Pro Plus tablet or caffeinated gel too.

I change into my race shoes at this point. It's a good idea to have done some running, preferably some long runs, in the trainers you'll wear for the marathon. And never a good idea to wear new ones fresh out of the box. I have many photos of disgusting blisters in case you need proof of that last point.

Next, the epic queues for the portaloos. It's just one of those things. Everybody is going to need to go at least once – at least.

Your phone: are you running with it and if so, have you practised with it in an arm holder, are you leaving it in your bag to collect when you finish? Decide in advance, it's one less thing to worry about on the day. If like me, you prefer to leave your phone at home, you'll need to have arranged somewhere for friends and family to meet you after the race – don't miss out on those well-earned congratulations just because your mum's on the Mall while you're looking for her in Trafalgar Square.

Speaking of friends and family, be sure to let them know if there's anything you suspect will annoy you while you're running and tired, and they're trying to be encouraging. I know people who dislike flippant comments mid-marathon – and are therefore sure to steer well clear of me. My personal view is to be grateful for any and all encouragement, even the comedians shouting 'nearly there' at Mile 4. Remember, even they mean well. Marathons now have apps to make it easier for people to follow your progress and find you on the course.

It's typically around 45 minutes between dropping off your bag and starting running. Do you have any old clothes you can wear and discard? There'll be big piles of clothes left on the start line of any marathon and they'll all be given to charity.

By now, everyone wants to chat. This is the culmination of months of training for elite athletes and happy amateurs alike. The nervous energy is intoxicating. I try to drink it in, taste it, feel it. This is what life's all about. And chatting to others and focusing on their training, their hopes, their ambitions stops me becoming too nervous about my own.

It all gets a bit serious with around five minutes to go. Into starting pens, last shoelace adjustments, perhaps a chance to visualise the race. Paula Radcliffe once told me to expect three things to go wrong. There will be highs and lows in any race as long as a marathon. A blister, a stomach ache, a sudden urge to poo. Or even the mid-race blues. I try to anticipate how I might react to these issues so they're less of shock if they happen.

Depending on which pen you're in, it may take a while to cross the line after the gun goes. It won't affect your time; marathons are all chipped now so the clock only starts when you cross the line. But do glance at the clock even so and try to remember what it says. Then when you pass other clocks along the way, at 10k, say, or halfway, you'll know how much time to subtract. Sure, you can always check your watch, but it's nice not to have to.

As you start running, there are people literally everywhere. I saw a pal drop his phone soon after crossing the start line in Paris. He had to bend down and edge backwards to retrieve it, with 40,000 people bearing down on him, tutting in French as he apologetically tried not to trip anyone up. He said it made the great African wildebeest migration – where two million half-tonne, horned, terrified animals stampede from the Serengeti to the Maasai Mara – seem tame. Don't drop stuff!

And watch out for bollards, road islands, pavements, street signs … With so many people running all around you, these things appear out of nowhere and it can seem that they're all out to get you. This is where running etiquette comes in.

If you see a potential hazard, it's just plain kind to call out to warn others: 'Bollard ahead!' 'Speed bump coming up!' 'High kerb on the left!' And as with every time you help others, it ends up making you feel better.

Similarly, at the aid stations. It's always nice to warn other runners with a shout or a hand gesture if you're planning to cut across the road. If you take a cup or bottle and don't need to finish it, offer it round before discarding (not during a global pandemic though, clearly). And do chuck it away mindfully of others – it's unpleasant to have a load of water, or worse, sticky sports drink, thrown over you as you run.

On a similar theme – smile, enjoy the day and thank the volunteers. This is my one top marathon tip for absolutely everyone. Because smiling isn't just nice and it doesn't just make you feel better, it actually helps you run faster. Eliud Kipchoge is the first man to run a sub-2 marathon. He famously smiles when the going gets tough – and we should too.

In 2018, researchers in Northern Ireland asked a group of 24 runners to wear a breathing mask to measure oxygen consumption and then complete four six-minute running blocks on a treadmill while smiling or frowning. The runners who smiled used less oxygen, ran more economically and had a lower perceived rate of exertion than those who frowned and those in the control group.

Noel Brick, lecturer in sport and exercise psychology at the University of Ulster, co-wrote the study. He told *Runner's World* at the time: 'When we make a facial expression, we may experience the emotional state we associate with the expression. We associate smiling with happiness or enjoyment, states that make us more relaxed, so when we smile, we are consciously trying to relax. By adopting the facial expression of frowning, however, we are experiencing an emotional state of feeling tense.'

It turns out runners are 2.8 per cent more economical when smiling than when frowning. Which is a good way to shave about five minutes off the average marathon finishing time.

A good way to add unwanted minutes to your finishing time is to start too fast. For the first few miles, it's easy to be carried along at the same speed as everyone around you. That's why it's important to start in the right pen. Don't be afraid of being overtaken. By a thousand people, if necessary. Or more. Remember, it's easier to catch up on your schedule than maintain your speed later on. This is the mantra I try – but often forget – to repeat:

In the first half of the race ...
- *if you think you're going too fast, you definitely are;*
- *if you think you're going at about the right pace, you're going too fast;*
- *if you think you're going too slowly, you're probably about right.*

Experienced marathon runners can 'negative split', run the second half quicker than the first. It's some kind of holy grail that I've never come close to finding. I'd quite happily take an even split, to be honest – running both halves in around the same time. And yet, however many of these marathons I run, I can't seem to stop myself going out too quickly and hanging on as best I can.

Big city marathons will have pacers, usually for every 15 minutes from 2:59 to, in London's case, 7:30. The pacers will run an even pace throughout the marathon and generally have a large group of runners around them. Many find it easier to leave the pacing to others and just hang in there.

Quite apart from the fact that the wind resistance is that much less if you're running in the middle of a big group, it can feel like you're on a train, just being pulled along towards the finish.

I've paced parkruns and half-marathons, once helping a friend to a visually impaired world record at the Windsor Half Marathon. It's enormously rewarding. But in a big city marathon, it seems the pacer can sometimes be forgotten in the moment. Another pal was once the four-hour pacer in London. I asked him how many friends he'd made, dragging people to a time they'd been dreaming about for months. The answer, it turns out, was none. Anyone who was still with him within half a mile of the finish simply used their last vestiges of power, sped up for all they were worth and left him and his steady, even pace to cross the finish line alone. If you do use one, please spare a thought for the pacer and be sure to thank her or him.

One of the reasons I sometimes start too fast is getting overexcited by over-exuberant spectators. A crowd can easily propel you to run too fast too soon. It's good to enjoy the crowds, and I'd always advocate running without music so you can soak up every scrap of atmosphere. But don't overdo it too soon. When you really need them, later in the race, that's when the crowds really matter.

Your own supporters especially. It's not always easy to spot friends and family when you're running. It's best to agree an exact point beforehand and to make sure you're running on the pre-agreed side of the road. And it really helps if they wave something large and colourful, so you've got something to look out for. Inflatable fruit works well – we favour bananas.

And from inflatable bananas to the dreaded Wall. Technically, this is what they call it when you slow down dramatically once your glycogen stores or your muscles' batteries run out. This is when you start rely on fat as a fuel source. The good news is, however skinny you are, you have enough fat to run on for days. And the bad news? It's horrible. Especially when you're not used to it.

I once ran an entire marathon at the end of an Ironman triathlon, through the Wall. The Wall that day was 26.2 miles thick.

Keeping those glycogen stores topped up through the race will help. Gels, jelly babies, glucose tablets, boiled sweets, they're all good. As are sports drinks, which will often be offered at the aid stations.

I sometimes train in a fasted state, doing my long runs early in the morning before eating anything, in a bid to practise using fat stores as fuel. Those runs can be truly ugly. But you know what the SAS say? … *Train hard, fight easy.*

Hitting the Wall can also mean a general feeling of cramp, exhaustion, overwhelm. Energy and adrenaline will be running low. This is the time for that well of willpower you never knew you possessed. Your determination will see you through, just guts it out – you've got this. And remember, if you think you're going to hit the Wall, then you probably will.

Oh, and the real halfway point is 20 miles.

Anna Harding is the presenter of The Running Channel. She once recorded her thoughts, mile by mile, while running the Brighton Marathon. The video has been watched half a million times on YouTube.

START
Standing at the start line. Obviously, need to wee, only just been – but definitely need to queue up for a wee again.

GUN GOES
Start Garmin … Whoo, let's do this!

MILE 1
Yay, Mile 1, feeling great!

MILE 2
Two miles gone, feeling great, but I think I've probably gone off a bit too fast.

MILE 3
Whoooo! One parkrun down, not sure how many left to go. Probably best I don't work it out.

MILE 4
Now I come to think about it, how many parkruns are there in a marathon…? Um, about eight and a half so it's about seven to go!

MILE 5
That was a really big hill, might have a gel soon. Give me something else to think about.

MILE 6
Whoo, six miles done! So, 20 to go. Hmmm …

MILE 7
Mile 7, only seven. Okay, that's okay. It's okay.

MILE 8
One step at a time.

MILE 9
I wonder if my cheer squad are coming up soon?

MILE 10
Mile 10, into double digits, yeah!

MILE 11
Time for some more gels … Do not hit that Wall.

MILE 12
I think I just saw … No, wait. I think I just heard someone say, 'Nearly there.' We're really not. That's not helpful.

MILE 13
Whoo, 13 – that's nearly halfway. I can see the halfway mark.

HALFWAY
I feel a bit of Bon Jovi coming on. Woa, we're halfway there… woa-oh, livin' on a prayer …

MILE 14
I wonder if the winner's finished yet?

MILE 15
Fifteen miles. When this is done, I am eating – all the food.

MILE 16
All these people cheering are amazing!

MILE 17
I'm sure these mile markers keep getting further and further apart.

MILE 18
Eighteen miles. Why does it feel like time has stopped?

MILE 19
Right, 19 miles. So, in one mile, I'll be five miles away from two miles to go, which is two miles away from … Hang on, Maths … In one mile, I'll be five miles away from being – done? In one mile, it'll be five miles to go, which is two miles away from being two miles to go, which is one mile away from being one mile to go? Which means it's nearly the end.

MILE 20
Twenty miles in … The real second half starts now.

MILE 21
'Run a marathon,' they said. 'It'll be fun,' they said. How can I be so near the end compared to when we started and still feel so far away?

MILE 22
*Everything hurts. (Sees a dog at the side of the road with
a 'good luck' sign round his neck.) Great cheering, puppy!*

MILE 23
Yay! Just a parkrun to go.

MILE 24
*I feel like I'm sprinting, but I'm not actually sure if I'm
moving forward or backward.*

MILE 25
*I'd really like to walk a bit, but there's too many people
watching.*

MILE 26
This is the best bit … I spy the finish line!

FINISH
*Don't forget to stop your Garmin. Everything hurts, but
that was amazing. Oh, my God!
It's windy out there. I need all the food, a coffee and
maybe a sit down.*

COLLECTS MEDAL
This makes it all so worthwhile.

And you know what? She's spot on about the medal. It always
feels wonderful to finish something as difficult as a marathon
and be given a tangible reward by a smiling volunteer. They

usually place the medal around your neck as you stand there on wobbly legs – which makes you feel like an Olympian.

And you know what?

You deserve that medal. I keep all of mine. Nothing worth having comes easy. And marathon medals, without exception, are hard-earned.

You lose body heat quickly after you stop running, so it's a good idea to put on a warm top as soon as possible. I'll usually leave one in my race bag, or ask loved ones to bring one along if they're meeting me at the finish. Many marathons often offer foil blankets – do accept one, they really work.

This is also an important time to replenish your reserves. Your body has taken a bit of a battering – a lot of a battering in many cases – and even if you don't much feel like eating or drinking, the sooner you can get some nourishment inside you, the better. Protein, isotonic sports drink, perhaps a flapjack … There should be a nice selection in your finish-line goody bag.

Many big city marathons keep you moving long after the finish line. In New York, it's an extra mile up and then back down Central Park. This is, counterintuitively perhaps, a Good Thing. It helps flush the waste products out of your muscles and reduces the dreaded DOMS – delayed onset muscle soreness – of the following days.

I find it also helps to find a quiet spot and lie on my back with my legs raised against a wall or barrier. Not only will it lessen the DOMS, but it's a lovely chance to reflect on my race. How did it go? Which bits did I enjoy most? What can I learn for the future? I try to remember to give myself a pat on the back too – I've just run a marathon after all!

Speaking of which, a celebratory drink – a proper drink – never tastes as good as it does after a marathon. My own preference is a cold, fizzy lager (a Peroni would be perfect, if you're offering). But I have running pals who enjoy a Guinness after marathons, others who like a nice glass of wine and several who hit the tequila – they don't seem to mind a sore head to go with their sore legs the next morning.

And yes, the DOMS. The day after a marathon, and sometimes even more so the day after that, it hurts to walk. Stairs down are a particular nightmare (best attempted backwards, by the way). I've occasionally attempted a run, but it feels like your thighs are made of jagged glass with every step. It's all awesome!

DOMS is your badge of honour. Unless you live in New York and have just completed your hometown marathon, it's unseemly to wear your medal any longer than the rest of Race Day. New Yorkers naturally wear theirs for a week but elsewhere, DOMS is your calling card that you've just run a marathon. That straight-legged, half-limp tells everybody who sees it how amazing you've just been. Not least yourself.

Because you know what? You *are* amazing: you've just run a marathon.

WHAT TO REMEMBER

- The less you leave to chance, the better your race-day experience;
- You'll be tempted to run too fast at the start, but please don't – you'll regret it;
- Smile! It makes a big difference, even when you're struggling. Especially when you're struggling;
- Remember to thank the volunteers at the aid stations;
- Try to anticipate how you may react to mid-race setbacks so they're less of a shock if they happen;
- A giant inflatable makes friends and family easier to spot among the throngs;
- The real halfway point is 20 miles;
- Keep moving through the finish line;
- The day after a marathon, enjoy your sore legs – you earned them ...
- ... but best attempt going downstairs backwards!

TRAINING PLANS

BEGINNER TRAINING PLAN

This training plan is aimed at novice marathon runners covering the distance for the first time, with a few tweaks and challenges if you want to test yourself, or if you feel like pushing on a bit, if your training is going really well.

The plan assumes that you will run three times a week and that you've done very little running in the past but are generally in good health and committed to your marathon journey.

The days of the week shown are not fixed and only proposed. If you change them, try to ensure that a run day is followed by a rest day (for example, run on Monday, Wednesday and Saturday or Tuesday, Thursday and Sunday).

DIFFERENT TYPES OF TRAINING RUN

EASY RUNS (Less Than 60 Per Cent Maximum Effort)
During an easy run, you should feel relaxed. You should be breathing comfortably and be capable of holding a conversation throughout the run. If you're a new runner, nothing may feel easy at first – slow down, walk if necessary and control your effort.

STEADY RUNS (60-70 Per Cent Maximum Effort)

These are the bread and butter of your training, the 'miles in the bank'. Steady runs build the base that is the foundation for the rest of your training. Conversations are still possible at this pace, but in sentences rather than long gossip.

TEMPO RUNS (70-80 Per Cent Maximum Effort)

Running at tempo pace is great for improving your running economy. It's a sustained cruise pace that requires concentration. You will find these runs slightly uncomfortable as you try to run faster, but they are worth it.

LONG RUNS

These are a real focus of the plan. They should be used to develop strength and endurance but also to practise your target marathon pace and control. Long runs are shown in both time and distance.

WEEK 1

MONDAY   REST DAY – Increase time on your feet and build a strong foundation and routine

TUESDAY   WALK 30 MINUTES

WEDNESDAY   REST DAY

THURSDAY   RUN/WALK 40 MINUTES – 10-minute brisk walk, 20-minute easy run, 10-minute brisk walk

FRIDAY   REST DAY

SATURDAY   REST DAY

SUNDAY   RUN/WALK 50 MINUTES – 10-minute walk, 30-minute easy run, 10-minute walk

WEEK 2

MONDAY   REST DAY – The first few weeks are important. Find the time to fit in your workouts

TUESDAY   RUN/WALK 40 MINUTES (10-minute walk, 10-minute run) × two

WEDNESDAY   REST DAY

THURSDAY   RUN/WALK 50 MINUTES – 10-minute brisk walk, 30-minute easy run, 10-minute brisk walk

FRIDAY   REST DAY

SATURDAY   REST DAY

SUNDAY   RUN/WALK 65 MINUTES – 10-minute walk, 20-minute easy run, 10-minute walk, 15-minute easy run, 10-minute walk

WEEK 3

MONDAY   REST DAY – You're doing a great job. The more you do, the easier it feels!

TUESDAY   RUN/WALK 40 MINUTES – five-minute walk, 30-minute easy run, five-minute walk

WEDNESDAY   REST DAY

THURSDAY   RUN/WALK 50 MINUTES – five-minute brisk walk, 40-minute easy run, five-minute brisk walk

FRIDAY   REST DAY

SATURDAY   REST DAY

SUNDAY   RUN/WALK 80 MINUTES – 10-minute walk, 30-minute jog, 10-minute walk, 20-minute jog, 10-minute walk

WEEK 4

MONDAY   REST DAY – The first block of four weeks is almost done! Stick to your plan this week and build up to your longest time on your feet

TUESDAY   40 MINUTES EASY RUN

WEDNESDAY   REST DAY

THURSDAY   RUN/WALK 55 MINUTES – five-minute brisk walk, 45-minute easy run, five-minute brisk walk

FRIDAY   REST DAY

SATURDAY   REST DAY

SUNDAY   RUN/WALK 90 MINUTES – 10-minute walk, 30-minute jog, 10-minute walk, 30-minute jog, 10-minute walk, or distance goal of six to eight miles

WEEK 5

MONDAY   REST DAY – A lighter week to allow for adaptation to the training loads

TUESDAY   20 MINUTES EASY RUN

WEDNESDAY   REST DAY

THURSDAY   30 MINUTES EASY RUN

FRIDAY   REST DAY

SATURDAY   REST DAY

SUNDAY   RUN 52 MINUTES – 25-minute easy run, two-minute walk, 25-minute easy run

WEEK 6

MONDAY   REST DAY – This week is when the marathon training kicks in, building more time on your feet and introducing some mixed-paced running

TUESDAY   40 MINUTES EASY RUN

WEDNESDAY   REST DAY

THURSDAY   RUN 40 MINUTES – 10-minutes easy run, (30-second tempo running, two-minute walk) × eight, 10-minute easy run

FRIDAY   REST DAY

SATURDAY   REST DAY

SUNDAY   RUN/WALK ONE HOUR 40 MINUTES – (20-minute easy run, five-minute brisk walk) × four, or distance goal of six to eight miles

WEEK 7

MONDAY   REST DAY – A solid week in the bank allowing training to settle and routine to continue

TUESDAY   40 MINUTES EASY RUN

WEDNESDAY   REST DAY

THURSDAY   RUN 40 MINUTES – 10-minute easy run, (45-second tempo running, one minute 45 seconds walk/run) × eight, 10-minute easy run

FRIDAY   REST DAY

SATURDAY   REST DAY

SUNDAY   RUN ONE HOUR 45 MINUTES – (30-minute jog, five-minute brisk walk) × three, or distance goal of eight miles

WEEK 8

MONDAY   REST DAY – This week, feel your heart pounding and your breathing quicken with the tempo running

TUESDAY   40 MINUTES EASY RUN

WEDNESDAY   REST DAY

THURSDAY   RUN 50 MINUTES – 10-minute easy jog, (60-second tempo running, two-minute walk/jog) × 10, 10-minute easy jog

FRIDAY   REST DAY

SATURDAY   REST DAY

SUNDAY   RUN ONE HOUR 40 MINUTES – (20-minute jog, five-minute brisk walk) × four, or distance goal of eight to 10 miles

WEEK 9

MONDAY   REST DAY – The next few weeks are all about the long run, building your capacity to run the marathon. Do not worry about covering the race distance before the event, just trust the training. Practise your hydration and fuel strategies on your long runs (see pages 189–200)

TUESDAY   40 MINUTES EASY RUN

WEDNESDAY   REST DAY

THURSDAY   RUN 30 MINUTES – 10-minute easy run, (four-minute tempo run, three-minute easy jog/walk recovery) × four, 10-minute easy run

FRIDAY   REST DAY

SATURDAY   REST DAY

SUNDAY   RUN TWO HOURS – (28-minute run, two-minute walk) × four, or distance goal of 10 to 12 miles

WEEK 10

MONDAY   REST DAY – Race practice: enter a half-marathon to familiarise yourself with Race Day routines, such as pre-race meal, race clothing and hydration strategies (see also pages 189–200)

TUESDAY   RUN 35 MINUTES – 10-minute easy run, (three × three minutes at a tempo pace with two-minute jog recovery), 10-minute easy run

WEDNESDAY   REST DAY

THURSDAY   30 MINUTES EASY RUN

FRIDAY   REST DAY

SATURDAY	REST DAY
SUNDAY	RACE – Race a half-marathon, or run for two hours 15 minutes, or distance goal of 12 miles

WEEK 11

MONDAY	REST DAY – The next four weeks are about getting to know your race pace. Have a target time in minutes and work out your pace per mile.
TUESDAY	45 MINUTES EASY RUN
WEDNESDAY	REST DAY
THURSDAY	RUN 60 MINUTES – 10-minute easy run, (five-minute tempo run, three-minute easy run/walk recovery) × five, 10-minute easy run
FRIDAY	REST DAY
SATURDAY	REST DAY
SUNDAY	RUN TWO HOURS 30 MINUTES (28-minute easy run, two-minute walk) × five, or distance goal of 14 to 16 miles. Include a few miles at target marathon pace

WEEK 12

MONDAY	REST DAY – There are just three more weeks of hard training left before the taper and you start to run less and sharpen up
TUESDAY	50 MINUTES EASY RUN
WEDNESDAY	REST DAY
THURSDAY	RUN 52 MINUTES – 10-minute easy run, (six-minute tempo run, two-minute easy run/walk recovery) × four, 10-minute easy run

FRIDAY	REST DAY
SATURDAY	REST DAY
SUNDAY	RUN THREE HOURS (28-minute easy run, two-minute walk) × six, or distance goal of 16 to 18 miles. Include a few miles at target marathon pace

WEEK 13

MONDAY	REST DAY – Dial in to your long run this week. Focus, plan and prepare. Relax, tune in and tick off the miles!
TUESDAY	50 MINUTES EASY RUN
WEDNESDAY	REST DAY
THURSDAY	RUN 50 MINUTES – 10-minute easy run, 10-minute steady run, 10 minutes at target marathon pace, 10-minute tempo run, 10-minute easy run
FRIDAY	REST DAY
SATURDAY	REST DAY
SUNDAY	RUN THREE HOURS 30 MINUTES (28-minute easy run, two-minute walk) × seven, or distance goal of 18 to 20 miles. Include a few miles at target marathon pace. Remember, people run at different paces so the distance covered will vary

WEEK 14

MONDAY   REST DAY – The long run is reducing in volume. Don't be tempted to do more or you risk being tired on the start line

TUESDAY   40 MINUTES EASY RUN

WEDNESDAY   REST DAY

THURSDAY   RUN 50 MINUTES – 10-minute easy run, (three minutes at target marathon pace, three minutes faster) × five, 10-minute easy run

FRIDAY   REST DAY

SATURDAY   REST DAY

SUNDAY   RUN ONE HOUR 34 MINUTES (45-minute easy run, two-minute walk) × two

WEEK 15

MONDAY   REST DAY – The taper is here. Doing less is all about recovering from the hard training so you can stand on the start line ready to do your best

TUESDAY   RUN 30 MINUTES – 30-minute easy run

WEDNESDAY   REST DAY

THURSDAY   RUN 50 MINUTES – 10-minute easy run, 20 minutes at target marathon pace, 10 minutes faster, 10-minute easy run × eight, 10-minute easy run

FRIDAY   REST DAY

SATURDAY   REST DAY

SUNDAY   70 MINUTES EASY RUN

WEEK 16

MONDAY REST DAY – You can only do too much this week. Relax, look back at your training and see how far you have come. You are ready!

TUESDAY 30 MINUTES EASY RUN

WEDNESDAY REST DAY

THURSDAY RUN 22 MINUTES – five-minute easy run, 12 minutes at target marathon pace, five-minute easy run

FRIDAY REST DAY

SATURDAY REST DAY

SUNDAY RACE DAY – Start sensibly at your race pace and stick to your race plan. Trust the training, smile and enjoy yourself – you can do it!

IMPROVER TRAINING PLAN

This training plan is for runners who may have already completed a marathon and are looking to improve on a previous performance. The plan assumes that you will run four times a week at the start of your training, you've done plenty of running in the past and you're aiming to improve your marathon time. The days of the week shown are not fixed and only proposed.

DIFFERENT TYPES OF TRAINING RUN

EASY RUNS (Less Than 60 Per Cent Maximum Effort)
During an easy run, you should feel relaxed. You should be breathing comfortably and be capable of holding a conversation throughout the run.

STEADY RUNS (60–70 Per Cent Maximum Effort)
These are the bread and butter of your training, the 'miles in the bank'. Steady runs build the base that is the foundation for the rest of your training. Conversations are still possible at this pace, but in sentences rather than long gossip.

TEMPO RUNS (70–80 Per Cent Maximum Effort)
Running at tempo pace is great for improving your running economy. It's a sustained cruise pace that requires concentration. You will find these runs slightly uncomfortable as you try to run faster, but they are worth it.

LONG RUNS

These are a real focus of the plan. They should be used to develop strength and endurance but also to practise your target marathon pace and control. Long runs are shown in both time and distance.

WEEK 1

MONDAY	REST DAY – The next four weeks are about building a base of easy running, building time on your feet. This will form the basis from which to introduce more marathon-specific training
TUESDAY	20 MINUTES EASY RUN
WEDNESDAY	30 MINUTES EASY RUN
THURSDAY	REST DAY
FRIDAY	40 MINUTES EASY RUN
SATURDAY	REST DAY
SUNDAY	60 MINUTES EASY RUN

WEEK 2

MONDAY	REST DAY – Continue to establish your routine. Find the time to get out to run
TUESDAY	30 MINUTES EASY RUN
WEDNESDAY	40 MINUTES STEADY RUN
THURSDAY	REST DAY
FRIDAY	40 MINUTES EASY RUN
SATURDAY	REST DAY
SUNDAY	70 MINUTES EASY RUN

WEEK 3

MONDAY REST DAY – The third week of the plan is important. The steady miles are setting the foundation for the rest of your training.

TUESDAY 30 MINUTES EASY RUN

WEDNESDAY 50 MINUTES STEADY RUN

THURSDAY REST DAY

FRIDAY 35 MINUTES EASY RUN

SATURDAY REST DAY

SUNDAY 80 MINUTES EASY RUN

WEEK 4

MONDAY REST DAY – Build up your longest run to 90 minutes at the weekend. This will be a real confidence booster for the rest of your plan as it kicks in

TUESDAY 35 MINUTES EASY RUN

WEDNESDAY 60 MINUTES STEADY RUN

THURSDAY REST DAY

FRIDAY 35 MINUTES EASY RUN

SATURDAY REST DAY

SUNDAY 90 MINUTES EASY RUN

WEEK 5

MONDAY   REST DAY – A lighter week to enable your body
to adapt to the training loads

TUESDAY   20 MINUTES EASY RUN

WEDNESDAY   30 MINUTES STEADY RUN

THURSDAY   REST DAY

FRIDAY   20 MINUTES EASY RUN

SATURDAY   REST DAY

SUNDAY   60 MINUTES EASY RUN

WEEK 6

MONDAY   REST DAY – This week you'll introduce
more intensity to boost fitness and build pace
endurance. Run to feel and listen to your body to
judge intensity

TUESDAY   40 MINUTES EASY RUN

WEDNESDAY   RUN 44 MINUTES – 10-minute easy run,
(60 seconds fast, two-minute jog recovery) × eight,
10-minute easy run

THURSDAY   REST DAY

FRIDAY   RUN 50 MINUTES – 10-minute easy run,
(five minutes steady, five minutes tempo) × three,
10-minute easy run

SATURDAY   REST DAY

SUNDAY   ONE HOUR 45 MINUTES EASY RUN or
distance goal of 10 miles

WEEK 7

MONDAY   REST DAY – Make sure you show a range of
pace during the sessions so you can maximise the
fitness benefits

TUESDAY   45 MINUTES EASY RUN

WEDNESDAY   RUN 40 MINUTES – 10-minute easy run,
(two-minute tempo run, two-minute jog
recovery) × five, 10-minute easy run

THURSDAY   REST DAY

FRIDAY   RUN 46 MINUTES – 10-minute easy run,
(eight-minute tempo run, five-minute steady
run) × two, 10-minute easy run

SATURDAY   REST DAY

SUNDAY   TWO HOURS 10 MINUTES EASY RUN or
distance goal of 12 miles

WEEK 8

MONDAY   REST DAY – Really attack your faster running
and embrace the breathlessness

TUESDAY   50 MINUTES EASY RUN

WEDNESDAY   RUN 50 MINUTES – 10-minute easy run,
(90 seconds fast, 90 seconds jog recovery) × 10,
10-minute easy run

THURSDAY   REST DAY

FRIDAY   RUN 47 MINUTES – 10-minute easy run,
(two × 12-minute tempo, with three-minute jog
recovery), 10-minute easy run

SATURDAY   REST DAY

SUNDAY   TWO HOURS 30 MINUTES EASY RUN or
distance goal of 14 miles

WEEK 9

MONDAY   REST DAY – A consistent week where you should be feeling the benefits of the training that is behind you and feel more confident, if a little tired!

TUESDAY   50 MINUTES EASY RUN

WEDNESDAY   RUN 56 MINUTES – 10-minute easy run, (four-minute tempo run, two-minute jog recovery) × six, 10-minute easy run

THURSDAY   REST DAY

FRIDAY   RUN 40 MINUTES – 10-minute easy run, 20-minute tempo run, 10-minute easy run

SATURDAY   REST DAY

SUNDAY   TWO HOURS 45 MINUTES EASY RUN or distance goal of 16 miles

WEEK 10

MONDAY   REST DAY – Enter a half-marathon race to familiarise yourself with Race Day routines, such as pre-race meal, race clothing and hydration strategies (see also pages 189–200)

TUESDAY   50 MINUTES EASY RUN

WEDNESDAY   RUN 45 MINUTES – 10-minute easy run, (three-minute tempo run, two-minute jog recovery) × five, 10-minute easy run

THURSDAY   REST DAY

FRIDAY   30 MINUTES EASY RUN

SATURDAY   REST DAY

SUNDAY   ONE HOUR 30 MINUTES EASY RUN or race a half-marathon

WEEK 11

MONDAY	REST DAY – Recover from your half-marathon. Continue to explore what your marathon pace feels like. Start to dial it in and feel more confident
TUESDAY	30 MINUTES EASY RUN
WEDNESDAY	60 MINUTES STEADY RUN
THURSDAY	REST DAY
FRIDAY	RUN 50 MINUTES – 10-minute easy run, 30-minutes at target marathon pace, 10-minute easy run
SATURDAY	REST DAY
SUNDAY	TWO HOURS 45 MINUTES STEADY run or distance goal of 16 miles

WEEK 12

MONDAY	REST DAY – Build the long run and focus on your target marathon pace, hydration and fuelling (see also pages 189–200). Plan these things in advance but don't panic if they don't go to plan!
TUESDAY	50 MINUTES EASY RUN
WEDNESDAY	RUN 50 MINUTES – five-minute easy run, 40 minutes at target marathon pace, five-minute easy run
THURSDAY	REST DAY
FRIDAY	35 MINUTES EASY RUN
SATURDAY	REST DAY
SUNDAY	RUN THREE HOURS – one hour easy, one hour steady, one hour easy or distance goal of 18 miles. Include six miles in the middle at target marathon pace

WEEK 13

MONDAY   REST DAY – This week you will do your longest run. Use this as a dress rehearsal for Race Day; eat your pre-race breakfast, wear the clothes you intend to race in, practise hydration and fuelling strategies during your long run (see also pages 189–200)

TUESDAY   50 MINUTES EASY RUN

WEDNESDAY   RUN 55 MINUTES – 10-minute easy run, (five-minute tempo run, two-minute jog recovery) × five, 10-minute easy run

THURSDAY   REST DAY

FRIDAY   RUN 60 MINUTES – five-minute easy run, 50 minutes at target marathon pace, five-minute easy run

SATURDAY   REST DAY

SUNDAY   YOUR LONGEST RUN – three hours 30 minutes or distance goal of 20 to 22 miles. Include a section, perhaps the final eight miles, at target marathon pace

WEEK 14

MONDAY   REST DAY – The long run will taper from here, but you will still need to maintain your paced runs during the week

TUESDAY   40 MINUTES EASY RUN

WEDNESDAY   RUN 40 MINUTES – 10-minute easy run, (60 seconds fast, 60 seconds jog) × 10, 10-minute easy run

THURSDAY	REST DAY
FRIDAY	RUN 50 MINUTES – 10-minute easy run, 10-minute steady run, 10 minutes at target marathon pace, 10 minutes faster, 10 minutes easy run
SATURDAY	REST DAY
SUNDAY	90 MINUTES EASY RUN

WEEK 15

MONDAY	REST DAY – Towards the end of this week your legs should find their spring again
TUESDAY	30 MINUTES EASY RUN
WEDNESDAY	RUN 41 MINUTES – 10-minute easy run, (five × 60 seconds fast, 60 seconds jog), three-minute jog, eight minutes at target marathon pace, 10 minutes easy
THURSDAY	REST DAY
FRIDAY	RUN 30 MINUTES – five-minute easy run, 20 minutes at target marathon pace, five-minute easy run
SATURDAY	REST DAY
SUNDAY	60 MINUTES EASY RUN

WEEK 16

MONDAY	REST DAY – Use any spare time to relax and put your feet up. Come Race Day, do not get too excited, set off at your race pace and stick to your plan
TUESDAY	20 MINUTES EASY RUN
WEDNESDAY	RUN 32 MINUTES – 10-minute easy run, 12 minutes at target marathon pace, 10-minute easy run
THURSDAY	REST DAY
FRIDAY	10 MINUTES EASY JOG
SATURDAY	REST DAY
SUNDAY	RACE DAY – You are ready. Good luck!

ADVANCED TRAINING PLAN

If you're an experienced runner and have completed a marathon before, this is the training guide for you. The plan assumes you will run five times a week. On rest days, you might also supplement your training with cross-training or strength work.

DIFFERENT TYPES OF TRAINING RUN

EASY RUNS (Less Than 60 Per Cent Maximum Effort)
During an easy run, you should feel relaxed. You should be breathing comfortably and be capable of holding a conversation throughout the run.

STEADY RUNS (60-70 Per Cent Maximum Effort)
These are the bread and butter of your training, the 'miles in the bank'. Steady runs build the base that is the foundation for the rest of your training. Conversations are still possible at this pace, but in sentences rather than long gossip.

TEMPO RUNS (70-80 Per Cent Maximum Effort)
Running at tempo pace is great for improving your running economy. It's a sustained cruise pace that requires concentration. You will find these runs slightly uncomfortable as you try to run faster, but they are worth it.

LONG RUNS
These are a real focus of the plan. They should be used to develop strength and endurance but also to practise your

target marathon pace and control. Long runs are shown in both time and distance.

INTERVAL RUNS
These include periods of higher-intensity effort or faster running interspersed with periods of recovery or rest. Resting between bouts of harder running means you can maintain the quality and pace of the effort.

FARTLEK
The word 'Fartlek' comes from the Swedish, meaning 'speed play' and Fartlek training is just that – rather than running a set distance in a set time, you 'play' with different running paces and distances until you feel you've completed the workout.

HILL RUNS
Running uphill will work your muscles in a different way to flat road running, so to avoid injury, you need to let your body adjust. Your legs will feel more tired than usual after hill running, so allow them to recover before your next session.

WEEK 1

MONDAY	REST DAY
TUESDAY	30 MINUTES STEADY RUN
WEDNESDAY	45 MINUTES EASY RUN
THURSDAY	10-minute easy run, two × (five-minute tempo run, two-minute easy run), 10-minute easy run
FRIDAY	REST or cross-train. Core and stretching exercises
SATURDAY	14-minute easy run, 10-minute tempo run, five-minute easy run, 10-minute hill run, 15-minute easy run
SUNDAY	ONE HOUR 15 MINUTES LONG RUN

WEEK 2

MONDAY	REST DAY
TUESDAY	40 MINUTES STEADY RUN
WEDNESDAY	50 MINUTES STEADY RUN
THURSDAY	10-minute easy run, three × (five-minute tempo run, 2.5-minute easy run) 10-minute steady run
FRIDAY	REST or cross-train. Core and stretching exercises
SATURDAY	15-minute easy run, 10-minute tempo run, five-minute easy run, 10-minute hill run, 15-minute easy run
SUNDAY	ONE HOUR 15 MINUTES LONG RUN

WEEK 3

MONDAY REST DAY

TUESDAY 45 MINUTES EASY RUN

WEDNESDAY 60 MINUTES EASY RUN

THURSDAY 10-minute easy run, 10-minute tempo run, five-minute easy run, 10-minute steady run, five-minute easy run

FRIDAY REST or cross-train. Core and stretching exercises

SATURDAY 10-minute easy run, 30-minute hill run, 10-minute steady run

SUNDAY ONE HOUR 30 MINUTES LONG RUN

WEEK 4

MONDAY REST DAY

TUESDAY 15-minute easy run, four × (five-minute tempo run, three-minute easy run), 15-minute steady run

WEDNESDAY 40 MINUTES EASY RUN

THURSDAY 50 MINUTES FARTLEK

FRIDAY REST or cross-train. Core and stretching exercises

SATURDAY 10-minute easy run, two × (15-minute tempo run, five-minute easy run), 10-minute steady run

SUNDAY ONE HOUR 45 MINUTES LONG RUN

WEEK 5

MONDAY   REST DAY

TUESDAY   10-minute easy run, eight × three-minute interval run, 10-minute easy run

WEDNESDAY   45 MINUTES STEADY RUN

THURSDAY   50 MINUTES FARTLEK

FRIDAY   REST or cross-train. Core and stretching exercises

SATURDAY   15-minute easy run, 20-minute tempo run, five-minute easy run, five × two-minute hill run, 10-minute easy run

SUNDAY   TWO HOURS LONG RUN

WEEK 6

MONDAY   REST DAY

TUESDAY   10-minute easy run, two × (two-minute interval run, one-minute easy run, three-minute interval run, 90 seconds easy run, four-minute interval run, two-minute easy run, five-minute interval run, 2.5-minute easy run), 10-minute easy run, five-minute interval run, 2.5-minute easy run), 10-minute easy run

WEDNESDAY   45 MINUTES STEADY RUN

THURSDAY   10-minute easy run, 25-minute tempo run, 10-minute easy run

FRIDAY   REST or cross-train. Core and stretching exercises

SATURDAY	10-minute easy run, five × 30-second interval run, 10-minute easy run
SUNDAY	RUN 12 MILES – 12 miles long run with four miles marathon pace at end

WEEK 7

MONDAY	REST DAY
TUESDAY	30 MINUTES EASY RUN
WEDNESDAY	REST DAY
THURSDAY	15-minute easy run, 15-minute steady run, 15-minute easy run
FRIDAY	REST or cross-train. Core and stretching exercises
SATURDAY	10-minute easy run, five × two-minute hill run, 10-minute easy run
SUNDAY	ONE HOUR LONG RUN

WEEK 8

MONDAY	REST DAY
TUESDAY	10-minute easy run, 10-minute tempo run, five-minute easy run (five × three-minute interval run, 90-second easy run), 10-minute easy run
WEDNESDAY	45 MINUTES STEADY RUN
THURSDAY	15-minute easy run, 30-minute tempo run, 10-minute easy run
FRIDAY	REST or cross-train. Core and stretching exercises

SATURDAY	10-minute easy run, 3 × (12-minute tempo run, three-minute easy run), 10-minute easy run
SUNDAY	RUN 14 MILES – 14 miles long run with four miles marathon pace in the middle. Practise health and nutrition (see pages 189–200)

WEEK 9

MONDAY	REST DAY
TUESDAY	10-minute easy run, six × (four-minute interval run, two-minute easy run), 10-minute easy run
WEDNESDAY	55 MINUTES STEADY RUN
THURSDAY	REST or cross-train. Core and stretching exercises
FRIDAY	RUN 40 MINUTES – 10-minute easy run, 20-minute tempo run, 10-minute easy run
SATURDAY	10-MINUTE EASY RUN, FOUR × FIVE-MINUTE HILL RUN, 10-MINUTE STEADY RUN
SUNDAY	RUN 16 MILES – 16 miles long run as two × (four miles marathon pace, four miles slower than marathon pace). Practise health and nutrition (see also pages 189–200)

WEEK 10

MONDAY	REST DAY
TUESDAY	10-minute easy run, 10-minute tempo run, five × (three-minute interval run, one-minute easy run), 10-minute easy run

WEDNESDAY	60 MINUTES STEADY RUN
THURSDAY	15-minute easy run, 12-minute tempo run, two-minute easy run, two × (six-minute tempo run, 90-second easy run), four × 90-second hill run, 10-minute easy run
FRIDAY	REST DAY
SATURDAY	30 MINUTES FARTLEK
SUNDAY	RUN 18 MILES – 18 miles long run. Practise health and nutrition (see also pages 189–200)

WEEK 11

MONDAY	REST DAY
TUESDAY	10-minute easy run, 12-minute tempo run, five-minute easy run, six × (three-minute interval run, one-minute easy run), 15-minute easy run
WEDNESDAY	45 MINUTES STEADY RUN
THURSDAY	30 MINUTES EASY RUN
FRIDAY	REST or cross-train. Core and stretching exercises
SATURDAY	10-minute easy run, five × 30-second strides, 10-minutes easy run
SUNDAY	RUN A HALF-MARATHON

WEEK 12

MONDAY	REST DAY
TUESDAY	10-minute easy run, three × (10-minute tempo run, two-minute easy run), five-minute easy run, five × one-minute interval run, 10-minute easy run
WEDNESDAY	60 MINUTES STEADY RUN
THURSDAY	45 MINUTES FARTLEK
FRIDAY	REST or cross-train. Core and stretching exercises
SATURDAY	10-minute easy run, four × (five-minute tempo run, two-minute easy run), five × 30-second fast strides, 10-minute easy run
SUNDAY	RUN 20 MILES – 20 miles long run. Practise health and nutrition (see also pages 189–200)

WEEK 13

MONDAY	REST DAY
TUESDAY	10-minute easy run, 15-minute tempo run, five × (three-minute interval run, two-minute easy run), 10-minute easy run
WEDNESDAY	60 MINUTES EASY RUN
THURSDAY	45 MINUTES STEADY RUN
FRIDAY	REST or cross-train. Core and stretching exercises
SATURDAY	10-minute easy run, 10-minute hill run, 10-minute easy run
SUNDAY	RUN 20 MILES – 20 miles long run. Practise health and nutrition (see also pages 189–200)

WEEK 14

MONDAY	REST DAY
TUESDAY	30 MINUTES STEADY RUN
WEDNESDAY	50 MINUTES EASY RUN
THURSDAY	10-minutes easy run, three × (10-minute tempo run, three-minute easy run), 10-minute easy run
FRIDAY	REST or cross-train. Core and stretching exercises
SATURDAY	10-minute easy run, four × 30-second fast strides, five-minute easy run
SUNDAY	RUN 22 MILES – this will be your final long training run. Practise marathon pace and health and nutrition (see also pages 189–200)

WEEK 15

MONDAY	REST DAY
TUESDAY	35 MINUTES STEADY RUN
WEDNESDAY	10-minute easy run, four × (seven-minute tempo run, two-minute easy run), 10-minute easy run
THURSDAY	45 MINUTES STEADY RUN
FRIDAY	REST or cross-train. Core and stretching exercises
SATURDAY	Three miles steady run, two miles tempo run, three miles steady run
SUNDAY	RUN 13 MILES – Practise marathon pace and health and nutrition (see also pages 189–200)

WEEK 16

MONDAY	REST DAY
TUESDAY	10-minute easy run, 15-minute tempo run, 10-minute easy run
WEDNESDAY	30 MINUTES STEADY RUN
THURSDAY	40 MINUTES EASY RUN
FRIDAY	REST or cross-train. Core and stretching exercises
SATURDAY	10-minute easy run, two × (five-minute interval run, 2.5-minute easy run), 10-minute steady run
SUNDAY	RUN EIGHT MILES – two miles easy run, four miles half-marathon pace, two miles easy run

WEEK 17

MONDAY	REST DAY
TUESDAY	30 MINUTES EASY RUN
WEDNESDAY	REST DAY
THURSDAY	20 MINUTES EASY RUN
FRIDAY	10-minute easy run, four × 30 seconds fast strides, 10-minute easy run
SATURDAY	REST DAY
SUNDAY	RACE DAY! Remember to stretch and warm down with a 15-minute walk. Eat and drink well (see also pages 189–200)

WHICH MARATHON?

At the time of writing, all marathons worldwide have been cancelled or dramatically altered in response to the coronavirus pandemic. London 2020 was a spectacular elites-only multi-lap race around St James's Park, while the rest of us ran 26.2 miles 'virtually' to get our medal. But we hope fervently that things get back to normal soon and marathons start happening normally again. There's not been much point in my writing this book if they don't!

So, assuming they do, the only question is: which one to choose?

UK

ABINGDON MARATHON

When: April
Difficulty rating: 4/10
A favourite among running club members in the south-east. Relatively flat, pretty countryside, and definite PB potential. They allow runners with buggies so this is where many of the buggy world records are set!

BACCHUS MARATHON

When: September
Difficulty rating: 7/10
A hilly, off-road fancy dress party, starting and ending in Denbies vineyard in the Surrey Hills. They offer wine at the aid stations. Lots of fun, and impossible to take it – or yourself – too seriously.

BATH MARATHON

When: August
Difficulty rating: 6/10
About 10 per cent of this is run in underground tunnels and the rest passes through the gorgeous city of Bath and equally stunning surrounding countryside. Organisers plant a tree for every 20 registrations.

BEACHY HEAD MARATHON

When: October
Difficulty rating: 9/10
If you were in any doubt about what you were getting into, the start – straight up a long hill out of Eastbourne – soon lets you know that this is going to be brutal. Three major climbs await that are even bigger, but the scenery, views and volunteers make all the burning in your thighs worthwhile.

BELFAST MARATHON

When: May
Difficulty rating: 5/10
The race takes in the four areas of Belfast – North, South, East and West – starting at Stormont and finishing in Ormeau Park. It's known for its vociferous local support, almost like each district is trying to outdo the others.

BLACKPOOL

When: April
Difficulty rating: 5/10
A flat, frequently windy, coastal marathon. The course takes in the Blackpool seafront, the Golden Mile, St Annes and Lytham. Potential for a PB if you're not unlucky with the wind.

BRIGHTON MARATHON

When: April
Difficulty rating: 4/10
One of the biggest and best UK marathons. Super organisation and atmosphere, more downhill than uphill, and a seaside finish. What's not to like?

CAPE WRATH CHALLENGE MARATHON

When: March
Difficulty rating: 10/10
An extremely challenging race, including a climb of 2,500 feet. The route is exposed and remote, through some of the most spectacular wilderness in the UK. The marathon passes the famous Stevenson lighthouse at Cape Wrath and incorporates a mid-race ferry ride.

CHESTER MARATHON

When: October
Difficulty rating: 4/10
Everyone I know who's run this race raves about it. A fast course on closed roads, a racecourse, a cathedral, ancient city walls, several bridges and a lengthy loop in Wales.

EDEN PROJECT MARATHON

When: October
Difficulty rating: 6/10
Cornwall's biggest running event. This is hilly, multi-terrain and beautiful. Comes with a free Cornish pasty and can of local lager to celebrate afterwards.

EDINBURGH

When: May
Difficulty rating: 4/10
Voted the fastest marathon in the UK, this sells out every year. A gentle, five-mile descent to start and a route that takes in the Royal Mile, Arthur's Seat, the North Sea coast and the oldest golf course in the world.

ISLE OF WIGHT

When: October
Difficulty rating: 7/10
A race that's been going since the 1950s! The route was changed in 2013 to a single lap through quieter roads on the prettier west of the island. Exceptional value, scenic course and the option to have your own drink taken to one of the aid stations.

JERSEY MARATHON

When: October
Difficulty rating: 6/10
This race has become an increasingly important part of Jersey's calendar – and a big tourist attraction, with over half of the runners coming from the mainland. An undulating, single-lap course on mostly open roads, with the police on hand to ensure safety.

JURASSIC COAST MARATHON

When: December
Difficulty rating: 9/10
The Jurassic Coast Path is one of my favourite places to run in the world. There's sea on one side and glorious downs on the other. But it's tough. Really tough. Conditions underfoot and overhead are often tricky and the marathon is almost 28 miles long!

LEICESTER MARATHON

When: October
Difficulty rating: 5/10
This is a popular and fast-growing race, starting and ending in Victoria Park and heading through the city centre and on closed roads through surrounding countryside. There are no major climbs but the final mile is all uphill.

LIVERPOOL ROCK 'N' ROLL MARATHON

When: May
Difficulty rating: 5/10
Albert Dock to the M&S Bank Arena (previously Echo Arena) via all the major Liverpool landmarks and loud music from local bands to keep you company along the way!

LOCH NESS

When: October
Difficulty rating: 6/10
One of Britain's best-loved races. Runners are bussed into the middle of the Highlands and follow the B852 back to Inverness along the banks of Loch Ness. A road race that feels like a trail run. Beware the hill at Mile 18!

LONDON MARATHON

When: April
Difficulty rating: 4/10
Easily my favourite of the six World Marathon Majors. Millions turn out to support the runners and their cheers carry tired legs all the way to the magnificent Mall finish. A fast, flat course, £60m raised for good causes and the best marathon runners on the planet competing in the same race as you – albeit a lot further up the road.

MANCHESTER

When: April
Difficulty rating: 4/10
This is the fast, flat, friendly marathon that's already becoming one of the biggest and most popular in Europe. Yes, it's the flattest marathon in the UK and perfect for a PB, but there's also something about this race, an X-factor, which means you finish at Old Trafford with a great big grin on your face.

MILTON KEYNES

When: May
Difficulty rating: 5/10
I ran the first-ever MK marathon, which had to be extended at the last second to go around a river that had burst its banks. It's since become a firm favourite for runners who don't manage to get into London through the ballot. Flat, well-organised, and it's always fun to finish in a stadium.

NEWPORT MARATHON

When: April
Difficulty rating: 4/10
Organisers claim 70 per cent of all finishers have claimed a PB on a route that takes in the city's iconic Tees Transporter Bridge and the coastal wildlife and medieval villages of the Gwent Levels. A relatively new race that's fast becoming a fixture on the UK marathon calendar.

RICHMOND MARATHON

When: September
Difficulty rating: 4/10
Three famous bridges, two Royal Palaces and one major river. Also, Kew Gardens, Hampton Court and Bushy Park. The race follows the Thames through London's leafy south-west suburbs with the ascent of Kingston Bridge about as close to a hill as you get!

SNOWDONIA MARATHON

When: October
Difficulty rating: 9/10
Entry is via a ballot and with good reason: you can't get
much better running scenery than Snowdonia. Three major
climbs along the route with an average ascent of 100 feet
every mile. Encircling Snowdon, this has been voted Britain's
best marathon – twice.

WINDERMERE MARATHON

When: November
Difficulty rating: 7/10
Set entirely within a UNESCO World Heritage Site, this is
another of those bewitchingly beautiful marathons. An
undulating, anti-clockwise circuit of Lake Windermere,
starting and finishing in Brathay Hall. Some of your fellow
runners will be completing the gruelling 10in10, so this will
be their tenth 26.2-mile circuit of the lake in as many days.

YORKSHIRE MARATHON

When: October
Difficulty rating: 4/10
Friendly and glorious, with distinct PB potential. High five
the vicar as you run past York Minster, enjoy the famously
warm welcome from the locals as you run through their
gorgeous countryside and don't forget to 'Do the Y' (you
know, from Village People's hit song 'YMCA') as you cross
the finish line!

EUROPE

AMSTERDAM MARATHON

When: October
Difficulty rating: 4/10
You won't be surprised to discover this is the flattest big city marathon in the world. What it lacks in gradient, it makes up for in charm. Highlights include running through the Rijksmuseum, past windmills, along the River Amstel and the big finish in the Olympic Stadium.

ATHENS CLASSIC MARATHON

When: November
Difficulty rating: 6/10
Historic, epic, unique. The original route from Marathonas to Athens run by the ancient Greek messenger Pheidippides. Not an especially easy, or indeed pleasant, route, but with the local support in your ears and the finger of history on your shoulder, you simply won't care. The finish in the marble Panathenaic Stadium, venue for the first modern Olympics in 1896, is unparalleled.

BARCELONA MARATHON

When: March
Difficulty rating: 5/10
From the Sagrada Família cathedral to the Camp Nou stadium, there's no shortage of landmarks to enjoy on the run. Streets are relatively quiet at the start, but there's a

carnival atmosphere by the time you run through Las
Ramblas to a vibrant finish in Plaça d'Espanya.

BERLIN MARATHON

When: September
Difficulty rating: 4/10
The fastest of the World Marathon Majors and venue for
most world records. The route changed in 1990, three days
before German reunification, to run through the
Brandenburg Gate and unite both halves of the city. One of
the truly great marathon finishes. Tears are often shed.

BUDAPEST MARATHON

When: October
Difficulty rating: 5/10
An evocative experience throughout. The race starts in the
statue-lined Heroes' Square, meanders along the banks of
the Danube and returns via several stunning bridges to
finish amid live classical music concerts.

COPENHAGEN

When: May
Difficulty rating: 5/10
The slogan seems to say it all, this marathon is 'All About
the Race'. Even the amateurs way down the field feel like
they're racing each other over cobbles and past the harbour.
You don't come to Copenhagen to soak up the atmosphere,
you come here to race.

FRANKFURT

When: October
Difficulty rating: 4/10
Another of those fast, continental marathons loved by club runners hoping for a PB. But this is also lots of fun, not least the final hundred yards, indoors on a red carpet, to cross the line in a raucous Festival Hall.

ISTANBUL

When: November
Difficulty rating: 6/10
The only race in the world spanning two continents. It begins in Asia before stampeding into Europe over the Bosphorus Bridge. Istanbul seems to seep into you as you run through it, all very grand.

JUNGFRAU MARATHON

When: September
Difficulty rating: 10/10
As stunning as it is challenging. Run alongside turquoise alpine lakes and through traditional mountain villages with the Jungfrau mountain as the constant backdrop. The soundtrack is provided by locals playing alphorn and ringing bells. The 4,000 entries sell out in no time.

MIDNIGHT SUN MARATHON

When: June
Difficulty rating: 7/10
The world's northernmost marathon. The year I ran, it was raining so hard, I could hardly see 10 yards in front of me, but under normal circumstances it's engagingly pretty scenery around the Norwegian town of Tromsø – and whatever the weather, finishing at midnight in broad daylight is totally magical.

PARIS MARATHON

When: April
Difficulty rating: 5/10
Mostly flat but for one sharp incline at around 20 miles. Some bits of the route are quite quiet, but who cares, you're running in Paris! The Eiffel Tower, Louvre, Seine, Notre Dame, a finish on the Champs-Élysées … yes, please!

PRAGUE MARATHON

When: May
Difficulty rating: 6/10
A fantastic way to soak up the enchanting city of Prague. The music festival runs alongside the route so you're never short of live musical encouragement. Revel in running across the Charles Bridge, but watch out for lots of cobbles.

REYKJAVIK MARATHON

When: August
Difficulty rating: 6/10
A picturesque waterfront course, some gentle undulations and the locals are genuinely thrilled to have you. The race kicks off festivities for the annual Culture Night, which of course is always best enjoyed on wobbly legs!

ROME MARATHON

When: March
Difficulty rating: 5/10
If you're struggling at any point, just look up – you can't help but feel inspired. They close the entire centre on Race Day so it feels like you're on a private tour of the Eternal City. There's so much to take in, you almost want to run round twice!

STOCKHOLM MARATHON

When: June
Difficulty rating: 6/10
Unusually, an afternoon start so it can get quite hot as you trundle round all of Stockholm's seven districts but the atmosphere is immense and thousands pack out the Olympic Stadium to cheer you round the track to the finish.

VALENCIA MARATHON

When: December
Difficulty rating: 4/10
Didn't get the time you were hoping for in Berlin or York?
Valencia is your safety net. The course is flat and the weather
is usually perfect. A not-so-secret PB-seeker's paradise!

VENICE MARATHON

When: October
Difficulty rating: 6/10
Tight alleyways, narrow canal paths, stunning squares and
many, many bridges. This is a point-to-point route, starting
in a small town west of Venice and ending in the city centre.
Afterwards, runners rejuvenate tired legs in the lagoon.

REST OF THE WORLD

BIG SUR INTERNATIONAL MARATHON

When: April
Difficulty rating: 6/10
26.2 rolling miles on CA Highway 1, from Big Sur to Carmel.
Towering redwoods, crashing waves, coastal mountains and
verdant pastures – and a pianist in black tie serenading you
as you cross Bixby Canyon Bridge at halfway.

BOSTON MARATHON

When: April
Difficulty rating: 6/10
The world's oldest annual marathon, one of the Marathon Majors and a real bucket list event for serious runners. Notable features include the 'Scream Tunnel', Red Sox fans fresh from a game and the dreaded Heartbreak Hill. Even getting to the start line is an achievement, you have to have run a fast-enough marathon elsewhere to be BQ – Boston Qualified.

CAPE TOWN MARATHON

When: October
Difficulty rating: 5/10
A sweaty sightseeing tour of Africa's Mother City. Table Mountain forms the backdrop but not, mercifully, part of the course. One of the first marathons anywhere to be 100 per cent climate neutral, with zero waste going to landfill.

CHICAGO MARATHON

When: October
Difficulty rating: 4/10
Like Berlin, this is a world record-friendly marathon. Start in Grant Park and follow the blue line through 29 neighbourhoods until you get back, 26.2 miles later. The blue line painted on the road is a feature of the World Marathon Majors – it's the shortest route to the finish.

GREAT WALL MARATHON

When: May
Difficulty rating: 8/10
The only marathon visible from space! Two lengthy sections on the Great Wall itself – and just the 5,164 steep, deep, stone stairs. Hilly throughout and beware the infamous 'Goat Track'.

MARABANA MARATHON, HAVANA

When: November
Difficulty rating: 5/10
Starting and finishing in Old Havana, a gentle lollop through the grand avenues and harbour. Twice. Charmingly chaotic start.

MUMBAI

When: January
Difficulty rating: 5/10
Run with Bollywood superstars and cricket legends in the biggest and richest mass participation race in Asia. It can be quite hot and humid. Helicopters hover just above you, capturing race footage.

NEW YORK CITY MARATHON

When: November
Difficulty rating: 6/10
A massive marathon with added New York razzmatazz. An undulating course through all five boroughs, each with its own character and charm, with five leg-sapping bridges and a sensational Central Park finish. One of the World Marathon Majors and the world's biggest marathon.

NIAGARA FALLS MARATHON

When: October
Difficulty rating: 5/10
Lots to like about this. The race starts in one country and ends in another – Buffalo, USA to Ontario, Canada. The roads were once described by Winston Churchill as 'the most stunning Sunday drive in the world'. And the finish is so close to the Falls, the spray can drift over you as you cross the line.

OUTBACK MARATHON

When: July
Difficulty rating: 6/10
Most of the course is on the Central Australian 'red earth' – bush tracks and soft-sand paths normally closed to the public. Almost feels like you're on a different planet. With the breathtaking Uluru as the constant backdrop.

REGGAE MARATHON, JAMAICA

When: December
Difficulty rating: 6/10
A pre-dawn start to avoid the worst of the heat of the day, so
the elite runners will finish before most people even wake up
on a Sunday morning. The rest of us are treated to good
vibes and lots of reggae music. The Finish Line Beach Bash
is legendary.

RIO DE JANEIRO MARATHON

When: October
Difficulty rating: 5/10
Watch the sun rise over the ocean as you chill on the beach
before the start. The course is mostly flat, in the shadow
of Sugarloaf Mountain, past the famous Copacabana
and Ipanema beaches. This is a marathon with a real
Brazilian buzz.

TOKYO MARATHON

When: March
Difficulty rating: 5/10
The first of the World Marathon Majors on the calendar, in a
country that truly loves distance running. The course is fast,
but for three bridges near the end. Organisation that's
second to none, with the most regimented and regulated
portaloo queues you'll ever encounter.

GLOSSARY

100 Marathon Club – Entry to the club is simple. Simple, but not easy. Just complete 100 (or more) races of marathon distance (or greater). And prove it.

Barefoot Running, Minimalist Running, Minimalist Shoes – After the publication of *Born to Run* in 2009, minimalist running became a big thing and the major shoe companies saw an opportunity to produce minimalist shoes. Essentially, depending on how minimalist you go, it's trying to mimic running naturally, with no big cushion under your heel. If I started running again now, I'd definitely do so in minimalist shoes. But I've thankfully not had a major injury in a while, and frankly, if it ain't broke, don't fix it.

Body Temperature – When it gets even a couple of degrees hotter outside, your performance can suffer because your body temperature goes up, so the more you have to sweat to cool off.

Born to Run – Kind of the sacred script of endurance running. In it, Christopher McDougall, a former war correspondent, suggests (or proves, depending on your point of view) that humans were designed to run in bare feet and that modern running shoes, with their lavish cushioning, actually cause many of today's running injuries.

Buff – Relatively cheap and brilliantly versatile. A tube of light-weight, stretchy material. Wear it around your neck as a scarf, on your head as a hat, even a bit of both to keep neck and head warm. Really useful in winter. And in summer, if you fancy, wrap it round your wrist to help wipe away sweat.

Compression Running Clothing – Socks, shorts, tops, arm sleeves … It's claimed that wearing very tight clothing can help performance. The controlled amount of pressure improves the rate of oxygenated blood going to your muscles and deoxygenated blood returning to the heart. There's evidence to suggest compression does help in the recovery process by minimising soft tissue damage.

Drop Bag – These bags are used for packing anything you may want to have access to just before and immediately after the marathon. In a point-to-point race like London or New York, organisers will transport the bag to the finish for you. Using them is optional – I don't tend to bother.

Eliud Kipchoge – The Kenyan great will forever be remembered as the first human being to run a marathon in under two hours. His time of 1:59:40 – a marathon time starting with a one! – didn't count as a new world record because it was a specially arranged event that used pacers. Kipchoge also holds the official world record – 2:01:39 – and won Olympic marathon gold in Rio.

Elliptical Trainer, also known as a Cross-Trainer – A stationary machine used to stair climb, walk or run without excessive pressure to the joints, decreasing the risk of injury. They're actually quite fun.

Emil Zátopek – Perhaps the greatest, most popular, most innovative runner of all time. Multiple Olympic champion, hero of

Czechoslovakia. More details in Hampshire chapter (see pages 103–111).

Energy Gels – Generally sickly-sweet concoctions which provide glucose (and usually fructose too) directly to your blood-stream as an easily absorbable form of carbohydrate to give you an energy boost mid-race. Some can feel the effect within three minutes while for others, it might take up to 15. Energy gels are effectively concentrated energy drinks so it's best to have a little water at the same time to dilute them – the body needs water to digest carbohydrate.

Expo – Most big city marathons have expos in the days leading up to the race. You go there to pick up your race pack and race number, then spend loads of time and money enjoying the expo experience – all manner of running-related stalls, shops and physio tables, often with inspirational speakers and the latest must-haves.

Fartlek Run – As fun to run as it is to say. Fartlek is Swedish for 'speed play' and that's exactly what this run is all about. Unstructured, it alternates between moderate to hard efforts with easy efforts throughout. Play with speed by running at faster efforts to the next lamppost, the end of the street, until you see 10 red cars, etc.

Garmin – There are other running watches, of course, but Garmin are the most common.

Gun Time/Chip Time – Gun time is the time it takes to complete a race from when the starting gun goes off. Chip time is the actual time it takes you to finish a race as the clock only starts when you (and your 'chip', usually part of your race number or attached to your shoe) cross the line. Unless you start right at the front with the elites, your chip time will be significantly faster. It's never slower.

Interval Run – Short, intense efforts, followed by equal or slightly longer recovery time.

Junior parkrun – Free, weekly, timed 2k run on a Sunday morning for four- to 14-year-olds; think all the good stuff about a Saturday parkrun, then multiply several times over.

Mantra – Many marathon runners find a mantra to repeat to themselves as they start to struggle. Preferably something short – and therefore easy to remember – and positive. It may sound facile, but it works.

Maranoia aka Taperchondria – A strange hypochondria that seems to affect marathon runners in the fortnight before the race. Everything seems to hurt, old injuries flare up, new ones manifest … Fortunately, these aches and pains, though they feel real, are largely imagined.

Nike Vaporfly – Controversial shoe designed by Nike and famously worn by Eliud Kipchoge to run the first sub-two hour marathon in Vienna in 2019. Discussed at length during the Amsterdam and Gadgets and Gear chapters (see pages 89–97 and 179–188).

Pacer – Most big city marathons employ pacers, experienced runners who stick to a constant speed throughout to help others achieve a certain time. There's usually one for every 15 minutes, from 2:59 to five hours, and sometimes beyond.

parkrun – A free, weekly, timed 5k run in a park near you on a Saturday morning. Founded in South-West London in 2004, there are now thousands of events worldwide, all staffed entirely by volunteers, bringing communities together and making them happier and healthier. Brilliant, just brilliant!

Paula Radcliffe – One of the all-time greats of distance running. World champion and marathon world record holder for 16 years.

PB (Personal Best) – Your best time for the marathon (or other distances). It doesn't matter at all to some people, but it matters a lot to others.

Plyometrics – These are exercises that involve an explosive movement. Skipping, bounding, jumping, hopping, lunges, jump squats, and clap push-ups are all examples of plyometric exercises.

Portaloos – The starting area of any marathon is characterised by long queues for the loos. You will need to go, you will need to queue, it won't be very pleasant by the time it's your turn. Best allow time for this when considering how early to arrive.

Running Gait – Basically, how you run. If we all ran 'perfectly' – think Mo Farah or Eliud Kipchoge – we'd all be a lot less injured. There's also evidence that keeping our heads up as we run, fully stretching the body's fascia system, gives us free, elastic energy. But as discussed in the chapter on Stretching and Injury Prevention (pages 139–150), it's fine to run however we do and to make the most of that.

Spine Race – One of the world's toughest endurance races: 268 miles along the Pennine Way, from Edale in Derbyshire to Kirk Yetholm, Scotland, tracing the backbone of England. Non-stop. Mostly in the dark. Carrying all your own kit. In the middle of winter.

Starting Waves – Almost all marathons start you in order of your projected finish time – fastest runners at the front, nearest the line, slowest at the back. This makes a lot of sense. Not only does it minimise congestion during the early crowded miles, but it's equally frustrating to be constantly overtaken by the speedsters in running club vests as it is to be wearing one of those vests and weaving in and out of the slower runners. Some major marathons like London begin from three different places simultaneously, while others like New York start runners off in separate waves. In New York, the quickest runners will have all but finished in Central Park by the time the people at the back of the final wave are making their way across the start line in Staten Island to the sounds of 'New York, New York'.

Taper – Marathon training tends to gradually decrease for the three weeks or so before the race. Hardly any running is done in the few days leading up the marathon to reduce the risk of injury and you hopefully arrive on the start line fit and fresh, bouncy and shiny.

Tempo Run – Tempos, also known as threshold runs, are run at – or slightly above – your anaerobic threshold (the point at which your body shifts to using more glycogen for energy). If you can talk easily, you're not running hard enough, and if you can't talk at all, you're running too hard. It should feel 'comfortably hard'.

Ultra, or Ultramarathon – Any race longer than a marathon. Usually 50 miles or more, usually over hills and trails, sometimes self-navigating. They're a delight. No, really.

Yasso – A Yasso is two laps of the track, half a mile, run as fast as possible. Named after the legendary American coach, Bart Yasso. He worked out that the average time for 10 half-mile repeats, in minutes and seconds, will accurately predict your marathon time in hours and minutes. So, a 2 minute 59 second average for 800m translates (spookily accurately) to a 2:59 marathon.

BIBLIOGRAPHY

Alexander, Vassos. *Don't Stop Me Now: 26.2 Tales of a Runner's Obsession*, Bloomsbury Sport, 2016

—— *Running Up That Hill: The Highs and Lows of Going That Bit Further*, Bloomsbury Sport, 2019

Bean, Anita. *The Runner's Cookbook: More Than 100 Delicious Recipes to Fuel Your Running*, Bloomsbury Sport, 2017

—— *The Vegetarian Athlete's Cookbook: More Than 100 Delicious Recipes for Active Living*, Bloomsbury Sport, 2016

Hobrough, Paul. *Running Free of Injuries: From Pain to Personal Best*, Bloomsbury Sport, 2016

—— *The Runner's Expert Guide to Stretching: Prevent Injury, Build Strength and Enhance Performance*, Bloomsbury Sport, 2020

Hutchinson, Alex. *Endure: Mind, Body and the Curiously Elastic Limits of Human Performance*, HarperCollins, 2018

Jackson, Lisa & Susie Whalley. *Running Made Easy*, Collins & Brown, 2014

Jackson, Lisa. *Your Pace or Mine? What Running Taught Me about Life, Laughter and Coming Last*, Summersdale, 2016

Karageorghis, Costas I. *Applying Music in Exercise and Sport*, Human Kinetics Australia P/L, 2016

McDougall, Christopher. *Born to Run: The Hidden Tribe, The Ultra-Runners, and the Greatest Race the World Has Never Seen*, Profile Books, 2010

Robinson, Roger. *When Running Made History*, Syracuse University Press, 2018

Smith, Ben. *401: The Man Who Ran 401 Marathons in 401 Days and Changed His Life Forever*, Bloomsbury Sport, 2018

ACKNOWLEDGEMENTS

Well this has been a ton of fun, mainly due to the following wonderful people. I'm very grateful.

Firstly, to my great friend and colleague Chris Evans, for coming up with the title on air one morning. I thought I was done with writing about running, but as soon as Chris suggested *How to Run a Marathon*, I knew I wanted to write it.

Not least because then I got to speak to loads of fantastic folk – the experts who gave their knowledge freely and willingly, and fellow runners who shared their amazing stories. In order of appearance, a big thank you to: Lisa Jackson, Kathrine Switzer, Nick Butter, Anthony Butler and Jessie Rix, David Cornock, Nick Rusling, Anna McNuff, Andy Humphries, Rob Owen, Roger Robinson, Susie Comstock, Martin Yelling, Paul Hobrough, Alex Hutchinson, Professor Costas Karageorghis, Rick Pearson, Anita Bean, Mark Kennedy, Andy Blow, Esther Newman, Hélène Guillaume, Judge Craig Mitchell, Anna Harding and Martin Yelling again for the training plans.

The team at HarperCollins are really ace, notably Ed Faulkner, Lydia Good and Sarah Hammond. Then there's

Holly Blood who is nothing short than an alchemist. Thanks, Holly for all your awesome suggestions.

And finally, the best thing about writing a book about running marathons – it's a great excuse to run marathons. So, to my phenomenal family, to Emily, Matthew, Mary and most of all to Caroline, thank you for putting up with me sodding off to spend yet more weekends trundling round yet another 26.2 miles.